Recognizing the Hero Within

Recognizing the Hero Within

Inspiring true stories of personal empowerment

Carol C. Lake

carolclake2@gmail.com

To my husband and daughters, who have walked every step of this journey with me

Table of Contents

Section 1 - Never Give Up

Section 2 - Courage

Section 3 - Finding Yourself

Section 4 - Resilience

Section 5 - Giving

Section 6 - Life Lessons

Introduction

These stories are for you, a reminder of the indomitable human spirit and the power of perseverance.

It's as if we each begin as a unique mound of lumber – each an unmatched mixture of redwood, oak and pine – with the sole responsibility of making the most of what we have to build the best life that we can. Then sometimes unfortunate events get in the way, making it more difficult than it needed to be. But it is left to us to maximize ourselves, to learn how to use the tools and resources that we do have in order to produce the desired outcome.

Following my accident where I was hit by a car traveling at 50 mph, I had many broken bones, a fractured skull and was thrown into a severe coma. The neurosurgeon told my parents I should be able to take care of myself, but not to expect a lot more than that. My parents wondered how they would pay the bills for additional care, if needed. I didn't hear any of these negative predictions, and by the way, they were all wrong.

After my accident, I fought and struggled and persevered with the strength of my inner fire to regain who I was and to grow into my future self. There were no traumatic brain injury support groups back then so I had to do it all on my own, and I never gave up. I embraced the challenges and they became stepping stones to my success. In the end I have lived a vibrant life, earned multiple advanced degrees despite my traumatic brain injury, and with my husband have built a successful and joyful family.

What I experienced motivated me to create this collection of positive stories for others who need to overcome obstacles. There is a way forward, you just need to discover it. We all have an equal opportunity to grab a hold of our lives and decide where to take it, even when it defies the odds of success. If at first you don't succeed, try a different route until you do.

You can do it too - this all starts with you.

Sincerely,

Carol C. Lake, M.B.A., M.A.

Chapter 1

Recognizing the Hero Within

Never Give Up

Never Give Up On Your Dreams

Let me tell you the secret that has led to my goal. My strength lies solely on my tenacity.

~ Louis Pasteur

My dream in high school was to live in a big city and be an international marketing executive. After that I would settle down with a wonderful husband and raise a family. I was a high achiever in high school, had an engaging personality, was well liked, and the world was my oyster. Why couldn't I have it all? If I worked hard and stayed focused, it should work. Unfortunately, this dream was demolished in April of my senior year in high school.

April 16, 1978 was the first day I can remember after emerging from my 14-day severe coma. I had been hit by a car speeding at 50 mph while I was crossing the street. I had two shattered legs, a broken pelvis and fractured skull. My eyes were skewed to the right – an indication of bleeding within the brain cavity and a severe coma.

My parents were worried that I might be paralyzed and might spend the rest of my life in a wheelchair. But the reality of the situation was far worse than that – I could be left mentally disabled because of the coma, I could be left in a permanent vegetative state... or I could die. My rating on the coma scale was a 4 on a 3 to 15 scale, with 3 being the worst. This meant that if I survived I could have permanent brain damage.

I had been released from intensive care a couple of days earlier and was now in a regular hospital room. Even though I was now awake, my neurosurgeon did not give my parents much hope that I'd be able to do much more than take care of myself. Plus I would probably have a permanent limp. But at least I was awake, and this day was a good day.

I had been in the hospital for two months with my left leg in traction. Once my left femur had a long rod in it to hold it together, I only had breaks below my knee so they let me out of the hospital with crutches. Whereas I hadn't felt any pain when I was in traction due to the after effects of my coma, the real pain started when I tried to walk again.

Soon after I got out of the hospital in June, I was valedictorian at my high school graduation. As I hobbled up on the stage with my crutches and note cards, I started my speech. "Always remember the simple things in life, enjoy life. Everyone here is alive, always remember how good life is." I received a standing ovation after my speech, and this was the start of my long journey back.

I was scheduled to start at State University of New York in September of that year. When my tutor had come to the hospital so that I could finish my English class and graduate from high school, she rated my overall cognition as that of a 12-year-old. If you looked at me, I looked normal, but my mind was in turmoil. There had been no therapy for my injured brain. What was really scary at that time was that I could pick up a book and verbalize the words, but I didn't understand what they meant. That is, unless I was reading a book for an elementary school student. The old Carol (pre-coma) was kind, had a 3.97 GPA in high school, was never stressed, had a lot of friends, and was very focused. The new Carol (post-coma) was still nice, was always stressed, got headaches, slept a lot, fought off depression, and found it hard to remain focused. My personality was different than it had been. Life was turned upside down and my old dreams were a thing of the past.

My undergraduate studies were enormously difficult. I was fighting short term memory deficits and cognitive issues all the way, but I eventually taught myself how to learn again. Graduate school was even harder, but I made it through with a lot of effort. Although my neurosurgeon had told my parents that I probably wouldn't be able to go to college, in the end I earned one Bachelor's degree and two Master's degrees. I had beat the odds.

When I started working in San Francisco, I had earned my degrees but fell a bit short on how to put it all together and work in a business where you had to respond rapidly. Everything wasn't as organized as it had been in college, and this was the real world – a world in which I needed to figure out how to excel.

Although my previously shattered legs left me with arthritis in my knees, I did not have a permanent limp. The greatest trouble, however, was with my memory. I was forgetting about many of the tasks I had been asked to complete. And even when I did remember to get some information from a given source, ten minutes after I retrieved that information I'd forget what I had just learned. I felt the same as I had during my first year in college, because I couldn't seem to remember a thing. That tormenting circle was back!

Depression came back with the memory failure, but this time it was different. I was more in control now; I knew where I had to go, and was closer to getting there, but just didn't know the route.

Over time, I came up with an effective method to recall and retain new information. At work I would always carry a pen and pad with me whenever I went to speak with anyone on a business issue. If I write things down I can remember what was discussed. I still do that today, and it works. I never gave up, always had a lot of drive, and this was the key to my success.

I have found that what I have been through sets me apart from others. I've experienced an awakening by way of a deep sleep. I don't take things for granted and I have learned that I can do just about anything I choose to do. My goals are realistic, yet high enough to motivate me to reach them. My goals are truly an essential part of me, of my life, for they are the means to furthering myself, to growing and learning and strengthening myself.

I have a wide breadth of accomplishments in my career as a senior financial analyst, operations manager and finance manager. After I met my husband I no longer wanted to travel the world as an international marketing executive, but I didn't give up on my dreams, I just altered them a little. Today I work at a University, my husband and I have three teenage girls, and we live in the East Bay of San Francisco.

Everyone has a story to tell and we all have our own strengths and weaknesses. I'm a good example of someone who faced a tremendous barrier and was still able to achieve success. I would be a different person today if my accident had never happened, and I'm thankful for what I have accomplished and who I am. I have a wonderful family and a professional life I'm proud of. What I truly discovered is that even if your initial dreams are disrupted by something unexpected, success is still possible. Never give up on your dreams.

Carol Lake lives in the Bay Area

Raccoon Eyes

You have the power to say - This is NOT how my story will end.

~ Christine Mason Miller

"Oh my gosh", an off-duty cop in Burger King yelled, as he watched a body being hurled upward toward the lit street lamp across the street. "Someone call an ambulance", a woman sitting in the booth bellowed.

Within minutes both customers, and the clerk still holding the bottle of cleaner in her hand, were outside looking down at the broken glass and pieces of the car wreck. The car had run over her while she was crossing the street at a crosswalk. In a fit of hysteria, the woman who had just sat down to eat her fries began to weep uncontrollably when she saw a petite, and bloody female body laying face up in the gutter. While the face was covered with blood, the woman surmised it must be a teenager.

Moments later the ambulance maneuvered its way through traffic, swerving around corners, the earsplitting siren warning anything ahead that moved to clear its path. Upon arrival at the hospital, medical personnel promptly initiated procedures to stabilize the patient.

Meanwhile, the head nurse faced the task she often dreaded, though she had done it many times - she had to call the patient's family. Carol had her state ID card in her pocket, so she knew whom to call.

The dim lights of the waiting room at Kenmore Mercy hospital created a grim atmosphere that echoed the weight of the worry and hope in the air. The Creccas had been called to the hospital in the middle of the night, being told that their daughter had been in a terrible car accident. They could hear the beep, beep of the heart monitor and the up and down swoosh of the respirator machine.   Mr. Crecca gripped his wife's hand tightly, with all the strength he had. They followed the resident doctor, walking as though their legs had suddenly become weighted down with lead as they neared Intensive Care.

Mrs. Crecca's snail-like pace stopped. She closed her eyes. Can I handle seeing Carol so helpless? I can't fall apart in front of her. Am I strong enough to be strong for her? Mr. Crecca squeezed his wife's hand and smiled a reassuring smile as though he knew what she was thinking. She nodded and stood a bit taller and resumed—with great effort—her usual confident stance.

Inside, it was at that moment that the seriousness of their daughter's injuries became real to them, seeing her lying lifeless upon the hospital bed. So silent and still,

Carol laid, with a tube inserted into her nose, her eyes closed, and a sheet draped over her petite body, positioned in such a way that exposed her bloodied and mangled legs. Due to the bleeding from her basal skull fracture, Carol's eyelids and the area around her eye socket were black and blue; the medical profession calls this "racoon eyes".

I felt a hard, and fast-moving object strike me, and throw me high up in the air. I heard a loud breaking noise in my legs. Volts of electricity seemed to vibrate throughout my body. Then I crashed to the ground. My body spun out of control. Excruciating pain shot through my head. Am I unconscious? Impossible. I'm dreaming. Why can't I wake up? I can't speak. I can't move.

Mrs. Crecca bent down and kissed her daughter lightly on her bruised face. She brushed away dirt particles that peeped through Carol's auburn hair.

I smell Mom's perfume. Chanel.

Then she turned away to wipe away tears that poured from her eyes.

Mama, please, please don't cry

Mr. Crecca tried to speak, but his words became jumbled and wouldn't leave his lips. He fought with his eyes that tried to fill with water and won. However, he couldn't mask the distress that dripped from his face as he beheld his daughter's broken body.

Dad, why are you sad? Daddy, I'm scared. I can't feel my body. It feels like it's been torn apart from me.

My family's scared. I hear my doctor tell them I might not be the same again. What's happened to me? Why won't they wake me? Hearing their voices makes me happy and sad. I wish I could talk to my family. I've got to wake up. The longer I'm here, the sadder they become. I see glimpses of light again. It's getting closer. I've never seen light so brilliant and bright. Grandpa? Grandpa Crecca is that you?

I don't know what's happened to me. I know if I return to them, my body may be paralyzed forever or I may be mentally impaired. Am I strong enough to accept the fact that I might not be able to trot gracefully across an open field in Spring, achieve my goals of being a career woman, wife and mother? Do I possess the fortitude to do whatever it takes to get my body and mind back to normal if need be? My body is perfect here. The skies are as blue as the bluebird, and the air is scented with the smell of lavender.

The Creccas fell into each other's arms. At times at the

hospital they felt helpless, for there was not much they could do to help their youngest child. But still, they stood over her, stubbornly guarding her like a treasure. They continued to joke with her and remind her that she wasn't alone. They felt their words would reinforce Carol's strength and will to fight. But they were all becoming impatient for good news. Everyone waited through the slowly ticking hours, never seeming to reap a reward for their endurance.

The closer I am to the light, the more peaceful I feel, Grandpa. I miss my friends. I miss school. I miss everyone. I've got to fight. I can't die. I have too much to live for and accomplish. Life is a gift I must celebrate and live to the fullest no matter what. Why are you turning my hand loose, Grandpa? Why are you walking away? The light is becoming dimmer and dimmer.

Two weeks later, my neurosurgeon pulled my parents aside and spoke with them. "Hello, Dolores and Vincent," Dr. Hallac said cheerfully. He noticed the pink had finally returned to Dolores' cheeks. They separated themselves from the rest of the group.

"Dr. Hallac, look at Carol...she's talking with people, laughing! Thank you so much for watching over her!" they both said.

Dr. Hallac smiled appreciatively, "Carol should be just fine," he said. "She may not be a 'straight A' student anymore, and may get B's and C's...but she should be able to take care of herself and live independently."

Dolores and Vincent glanced at each other with slow, dragging smiles, and were puzzled by his comment but excused the concerning thoughts. One day at a time, they told themselves once again. Today is a good day.

After everyone left the hospital, Carol breathed a sigh of relief. Things had been moving fast, which caused her head to spin. She tried to get up out of her bed, but her legs wouldn't allow her to.

Where is everyone? What am I doing here? Then she remembered the young accident victim her nurse was talking about. She didn't think to ask the nurse the victim's name, age, and gender. No one could see her watery raccoon eyes.

Carol Lake lives in the Bay Area

Starting Over

If there is one thing that can be forecast with confidence, it is that the future will turn out in unexpected ways.

~ Peter F. Drucker

My life changed in a moment. While returning from taking my son and his friend to school, a car crashed into my SUV, causing it to roll. It took the Jaws of Life to remove me from the vehicle, and I remember nothing.

When I woke up in the hospital, I didn't know who I was. I didn't recognize my son or have any knowledge of current events. Who was the President? It was more like what is a President?

I had suffered a traumatic brain injury, which left me with retrograde and anterograde amnesia. My past was totally gone. Doctors told me that my condition was the best it would ever be. A therapist later told me to think of it as if I were a newborn, learning everything from scratch.

Life didn't get easier after being released from the hospital. Day-to-day activities were confusing. Basics like dirty dishes going into the dishwasher and clothes being inside the closet were new concepts. Meanwhile, I had my youngest child, a thirteen-year-old son, to raise. I was trying to learn the duties required of a mother in addition to the basics of functioning at home and in society, and it felt overwhelming. One day, I burned cookies when the kitchen timer in my pocket went off.... while I was standing in line at the post office. But give up? Never!

My motor skills were impaired, so I was constantly running into doorways. I thought "I must be huge!" In reality. I wasn't going through the center of the doorway like I thought I was. I had little feeling on my left side, so there were confusing signals from my brain to my body parts. Pain was ever-present. The rest of my life will always include chiropractic, physical therapy, therapeutic massage, doctors, and believing in my instincts.

Prior to my accident, I ran my own consulting firm specializing in accounting and database management. Returning to consulting was not an option; I would have no idea how to help my clients. In fact, trying to relearn even simple math was a challenge because I couldn't remember the number four – a common problem with my type of brain injury.

I began volunteering for my local hospital's auxiliary, editing the newsletter and raising money. Volunteering helped me learn what functions I was good at and which activities I wasn't able to do.

Friends encouraged me to enroll at Claremont Graduate University, where I earned a certificate in leadership. After lots of hard work, and with the help of patient professors and student-led study groups, I earned my master's degree in management with honors. While at the university, I became a student of Peter F. Drucker, the prominent author and educator. I was fortunate to become friends with him and his wife Doris. They encouraged and inspired me.

While earning my master's degree, I became director of the MBA program at the Peter F. Drucker School of Management. I found my rhythm as a productive, effective team member – bringing alumni, staff, students, and Professor Drucker together for the enrichment of all.

At some point during my journey, I decided to sculpt a personality for myself because I couldn't remember my character traits from before the accident. Based on observing others, I realized that if I became known as a happy person, people would want to be around me. From then on, becoming happy in spite of my circumstances was my mission. It became what I call my "happiness project."

As I focused on being happy, the key was not to dwell on the negative aspects of my life. For example, I made a conscious decision not to lament the absence of special memories, like giving birth to my children. Instead, I concentrated on the present.

I also became determined not to let setbacks destroy my happiness. When I was involved in a second car crash, I suffered another brain injury. It happened as I was finishing my master's degree, and schoolwork was much harder after this second injury. But I decided that happiness is a choice, and I just needed to make a conscious effort to stay positive.

In recent years, I have become focused on speaking, writing, and coaching, to empower people to break through self-imposed barriers, implement new strategies, and achieve successful outcomes, just as I have. I have founded a non-profit organization (www.tbibridge.org) that provides resources for survivors of traumatic brain injury and post-traumatic stress disorder. My motto is "Believe. Be patient. Never give up!"

My life now is rich with close friends, family and activities I enjoy, in addition to my non-profit work. I don't know what my life was like before the accident, but all that matters is I'm happy now. Attitude truly is everything!

Celeste Palmer lives in Claremont, CA

Chapter 2

Recognizing the Hero Within

Courage

Deposition

*Courage gives us a voice and compassion gives us an ear.
Without both, there is no opportunity for empathy and
connection.*

~ Brene Brown

I have been trained my entire life to be nice, cooperative
and helpful. Ever since I can remember, all my teachers
and neighbors thought I was such a nice girl: smart,
bright and a real positive force in the world.

One day, some 30 years into my career, I was called to
be a key witness in an important deposition, where we
were suing a consulting company for sub-par work they
provided that caused us to lose a lot of money. A
deposition is a part of the discovery part of a trial, in
order to find out more about the case before it goes to
trial. It is the taking of an oral statement by a witness
under oath, is recorded by a court-recorder, and in my
case, also by video.

The venue for this exercise was a large conference room
in our lawyers' office. The polished white table was
covered with laptops, cords, recording devices and
many papers and journals. It was very professional,
with everyone well-groomed and dressed in suits. There

were three lawyers on my side, two opposing attorneys, and a court reporter.

This case had a lot on the line, and it was very important for me to give the best deposition that I could. After all, our side was right, and it was my job to prove that we were right. I felt a lot of weight sitting on my shoulders, but I knew that with enough focus I could succeed. I'm an honest person and I do a good job.

"Do you understand that you are still under oath?"

"Yes."

"OK, let's continue."

This was hour five of what ended up being a 16-hour deposition. Two full, 8-hour days of the opposing attorney drilling me, quizzing me, talking fast and in complex sentences with disjointed thoughts, trying to get me to say the wrong thing.

During this time, my courage, steadfastness, strength, and professional demeanor were all being tested. I had to constantly focus during this period, never backing down and staying on the offensive. My strategy was to answer the question the opposing attorney was asking, no more, no less, just answer the question.

"I'm sorry, can you rephrase that last sentence in another way? I don't understand the question."

"Yes, yes, I'm sorry, let me try that again."

This young, aggressive defense attorney, who was new to the big stage and was out to make his mark, was hoping to show that I was incompetent. His goal was to get me talking and have me say something that they could later use against me at trial. He started out being very brusque with me and talking down to me in a harsh manner. Luckily, this had exactly the opposite impact on me – I was not about to let this snotty little lawyer win, and as he threw statements at me, I spat the answers right back at him.

It's funny, when I read on the internet about the particular actions taken in a deposition, I learned that the deposing attorney's job is to put deponents at ease in the beginning of the deposition. This is so that the witness will give up information freely, without the opposing counsel having to browbeat them for every answer. Well, I guess my opposing attorney didn't do the same research I did, because he didn't follow this standard protocol.

After the first break, however, the opposing attorney changed his tactics and was calmer. He still tried to confuse me by skipping back and forth with questions between different time periods, hoping that I would say something wrong. But it didn't work – I stayed strong and gave a really good performance.

This drilling lasted for 16 hours. It was excruciating to have every word on my resume examined with a microscope – yes that was a promotion I received and yes, that was a lateral move I made in order to broaden my experiences. The opposing attorney was trying to tear me apart and make me out to be a bad person. He was insinuating a lot of negative things about my character in the way he was asking his questions.

"The job description states, 'The incumbent is expected to serve as a subject matter expert'. Were you a subject matter expert?"

"I had a lot of similar experiences that allowed me to grasp the material quickly; I learned the specific expertise for the position on the job."

"So you were not a subject matter expert when you joined, correct? You had no experience with this specific business?"

I am a seasoned professional and have a lot of varied experiences. A job description is written in a broad manner in order to attract a wide variety of candidates with different backgrounds. I was not an expert when I joined, but who is? Why was he putting me down when it should be strictly professional? This two-day ordeal was a very humiliating experience. The slimy lawyer was trying to tear me apart, piece by piece.

The court reporter was a woman in her 30's, and her eyes and my eyes met at the end of each 1-hour session. She gave me a sympathetic look each time, and I could feel the warm wishes from her through her eye gestures. This helped me retain my confidence in the face of this emotional battery.

I'm competitive by nature, and I feel I "won" in this deposition battle. I didn't let the nasty little lawyer get the better of me, but rather stayed composed and did pretty well in answering only the question that was being asked. I felt like I was performing on stage, with all the participants listening intently to what I was saying. I was in the spotlight, in the starring role. If I did my job perfectly it was a good performance; however there was a lot of room for error and falling flat on my face.

For the most part I'm the same as I ever was: a nice, cooperative, and helpful person. However in the wake of my deposition experience I realized there are more facets to my personality than I imagined. I am also a strong, unflappable, and professional woman able to withstand incredible amounts of stress.

I also learned what a difference it can make in a person's life to see signs of empathy and solidarity from a fellow human being. The court reporter who worked at my deposition was completely professional as she carried out her duties. However, she was also sensitive to the pain and humiliation I was feeling, and she showed that. Just knowing that someone else in the room witnessing my struggle was enough to keep me going. I hope that if I ever see someone else in a similarly stressful situation, I would offer my support whether that person was a friend or a stranger. I know from experience how precious the gift of empathy can be.

Carol Lake lives in the Bay Area

My Superhero Enzo

Dogs have a way of finding people who need them and filling a space we didn't even know we had

~ Thom Jones, American Writer

Like Superman, the crime fighting superhero with extraordinary abilities Enzo flew around the world to join our family. A Belgian Malinois, Enzo came from the Netherlands with a badge on his chest, passport, collar, and leash. He is trained in search and rescue and is a canine officer in our local police department.

The Belgian Malinois, first bred in Belgium to be herders in the 1800's are an energetic and highly intelligent breed often found in both the military and law enforcement. They have a sleek and athletic build with a short coat that can be a rich fawn to mahogany in color. Their black ears and mask accentuate expressive and questioning eyes. Playful, protective, powerful, and alert they have a keen sense of smell, dexterity, and a strong drive. Like most Malinois, Enzo has formed an unbreakable bond with his handlers and is eager to please. This is the story of how Enzo, a police dog at night became my therapy dog by day and rescued me following my traumatic brain injury.

My name is Suzanne and I am a teacher who taught third grade for many years. The year Enzo arrived I was preparing for the beginning of a new school year in the middle of the recent Covid pandemic. Feeling excited and prepared to officially meet my new class of third graders online the next day, I decided to take a walk along the shore of the beautiful Carquinez Strait in my hometown. In one step, I tripped and fell slamming my head upon the pavement and my life changed forever.

Stunned, I was unable to speak. My vision, mobility, cognitive skills, processing and memory were greatly affected and my way of being in the world was challenged. In the beginning my injuries were visible: a swollen blackened eye, multiple stitches on my head, black and blue bruises on my face. I was told by doctors at the hospital I would survive and should fully recover within a few months. I was told I could even return to teaching.

It took several months and many evaluations by neurologists and speech pathologists to realize the extent of my injuries, many of which were invisible. Among my many injuries I had damaged my broca, the language center of the brain and suffered from: Dysarthria - difficulty speaking clearly because of weakness, slowness or lack of coordination in the muscles of the mouth, face, voice, and lungs; Anomic

Aphasia - difficulty with word retrieval; and Verbal Apraxia - unable to execute my words, leading to distorted words, rhythms, and inflections. Unable to express myself I felt like I had to learn how to speak again as if for the first time.

Isolated with my family due to the pandemic and forced to take early retirement due to my injuries, I withdrew and became sad and depressed. The longer my brain injury symptoms continued, the more lost and confused I felt. Nothing seemed easy anymore. Everything was a struggle, a challenge. I felt confused and uncertain of who I was. It was like a part of me had died.

I began rehabilitation therapy for traumatic brain injury patients which included: speech, physical, occupational, vision, and cognitive therapies for over two years. Embarrassed by my speech and language difficulties I rarely spoke and did my speech and language homework exercises in private until one day Enzo heard me making silly sounds: ba, ba, ba, ba, ba, ta, ta, ta, la, la, la and joined me. Enzo made a great audience. He loved it when I made silly speech sounds, practiced word lists and tongue twisters, and read aloud to him often wagging his tail rhythmically to the beat. He didn't mind that I was reading baby board books like *Jamberry* by Bruce Degan: "One berry, two berry, pick me a blueberry" or Bill Martin's book *Brown Bear, Brown Bear, What Do You See?* He didn't care when I stuttered, lost my place, or struggled to read aloud challenging words. He would just snuggle closer and put his head in my lap. Day after day he sat at my side and listened patiently as I pet and scratched his belly and read aloud. Soon I discovered that Enzo had favorite books. He loved poetry, especially children's poetry and would sometimes make sounds with the rhythm of the words. His favorite being *Be Glad Your Nose Is On Your Face* by Jack Prelutsky. If Enzo did not like a book, he would use his paw to move the book away or knock it out of my hand. Enzo brought me comfort, relieved my anxiety, my fear, and made me laugh. When I was with him, I would many times forget about my injuries and bask in his company.

Gradually my speech began to improve and I gained confidence. I began talking, telling my family and friends about my adventures with Enzo, my superhero - a police dog by night and my therapy dog by day who helped me transition and accept my life following a post traumatic brain injury.

Suzanne James-Peters lives in the Bay Area

A Sign of Bravery

Do you know what a foreign accent is? It's a sign of bravery.

~ Amy Chua

I've often heard that the best way to learn a new language is to move to the country where the language is spoken. The idea is that even a total novice will learn quickly when totally immersed in a foreign language. When I decided somewhat impulsively to live in Mexico as a young adult, I was very excited at the idea of improving my Spanish.

Improve it did! At first I was constantly confused, but as the months passed I became more and more dexterous at the language. I also managed to pick up cultural knowledge, such as commonly understood hand signs. For example, if one touches their elbow when discussing a third party the speaker is quietly implying that the object of the conversation is a cheapskate. No one ever taught me that in Spanish class, and I was pretty clueless when I first saw this in person.

Here's something else that no one ever tells you about language immersion: it's EXHAUSTING. I had no idea what a challenge it would be until I had to take my meager Spanish vocabulary and make myself understood by (and understand in turn) immigration officials, shopkeepers, tour guides, waiters, food vendors, ticket sellers, taxi drivers, beggars, neighbors, landlords and every other type of person you could come across in your daily life. Not only was I constrained by my limited knowledge of the language, but I was also confronted by the varying Spanish accents of people originally from other states, other Spanish speaking countries, and local indigenous people speaking Spanish as a second or third language.

Midway through my time in Mexico, I flew back to the states to attend a cousin's wedding. As I walked through a US airport to catch my connection, I heard an announcement made over the loudspeaker and almost wept in relief. For the first time in long months, I immediately understood the message without having to examine the speech in a deliberate fashion. I also understood the speaker's southern accent as well as the small joke he made. This information was all processed by my brain almost instantaneously and it really made me realize how labor intensive it was to acquire a working knowledge in a non-native language. As much as I missed my new life in Mexico, it was really wonderful to be surrounded by familiar sights and sounds for a weekend. This experience really fostered a greater appreciation for the sacrifices my immigrant parents made in building a life for themselves in the United States. They both came to the United States as adults, and because they have different native languages, their second language of English became the medium by which they communicated with their spouse, raised their children, and navigated both their professional and personal lives.

I recall feeling frustrated whenever I was called upon to explain jokes to my parents. They were often befuddled by jokes that relied upon English-language puns or knowledge of American pop culture, and I felt like by the time I explained why it was funny, all the humor had gone out of the dang thing.

There was also the matter of my father's "Talking to Americans" voice which embarrassed me to no end. My father's grasp of English is excellent; he's well read on a variety of subjects and has an extensive vocabulary across many subjects. Still, any time he spoke to a stranger, he would put on a deeper voice and over-enunciate everything he said. I spent countless hours trying to convince him that in America the correct way to say "wh" words like "what" and "where" means **not** pronouncing the "h". I would cringe to hear my father ask a salesperson "Where can I find this item? If you don't have that in stock, what would you recommend instead?"

Now that I've had a small taste of what it's like to struggle with a second language, I understand what my dad must have been feeling. It's so difficult to be taken seriously by others when you can't communicate effectively in their language. Conducting business in an unfamiliar culture makes a person feel vulnerable and at the mercy of strangers. No wonder my father went to great lengths to appear confident and well-spoken. He just didn't realize that clinging to outdated rules of pronunciation only highlighted the fact that he's a non-native English speaker.

I'll be the first to admit that I'm not as brave as my parents. After having traveled and lived in non-English speaking countries, I know there's no way I would ever build a life in a place where I don't speak the language fluently. I'm still flabbergasted that my parents made this sacrifice and more in their pursuit of the American dream. Amy Chua of "Tiger Mom" fame has something really insightful to say about this. Amy's stance on accents is:

"Do you know what a foreign accent is? It's a sign of bravery."

JB lives in Oakland,

Destination: Unknown

I love it when people doubt me. It makes me work harder to prove them wrong.

~ Derek Jeter

Looking back on my childhood, I'm struck by the feeling that I spent it longing for my adult life to begin. Above all I wanted to travel; to step on an airplane or ship and be transported to a faraway place with new sights, smells and sounds. Certainly this desire was not borne of experience, as my parents didn't have the time or the money to take the family outside of the greater metropolitan area. We were so poor that most of my childhood was spent in a multi-generational household of 6 adults and 2 children, all squeezed into a 3-bedroom townhouse. Life in such close quarters inevitably led to chaos, and I escaped by reading. My parents' prized encyclopedia set included entries about various cities and countries all over the world, which I voraciously devoured. I vowed that someday I would see the Taj Mahal, climb Mt Kilimanjaro, and sun myself on Hawaiian beaches. I was not shy about announcing my desire to leave my hometown, but adults in my life didn't seem to share this vision of my future.

I confided my desire to travel to my eighth-grade

English teacher. She was a vivacious person and had captivated her classes with tales of her adventurous life in the Peace Corps. I felt a sense of kinship with her and imagined that someday I'd enjoy similar trips myself. I remember how eagerly I gushed about my list of countries to visit and the details I'd read in preparation for future trips. After I finished speaking there was a pregnant pause. Searching her face, I got the feeling that she was trying to find a way to break bad news to me. Finally she said, "You know...you don't strike me as the type of person that will ever travel very far. I think you'll probably end up living around here all your life."

This pronouncement was delivered kindly, but I was devastated. I had the horrifying sensation that a sophisticated traveler had seen into my soul and found me wanting. I began to truly believe that I didn't have the "right stuff" for the life I wanted. In high school, I briefly considered applying to NYU, until my father scoffed that we could never afford such an expensive school. I immediately believed him and decided not to even put in an application. At his behest, I only applied to my local state university system. I received an acceptance letter to a school halfway across the state, but my parents felt that I wasn't independent enough for that. On their advice I attended a campus only a two-hour drive away from my hometown.

This pattern continued until my last semester of college. I was in the process of making my post-graduation plans. The practical thing to do would be to move back to my parents' house and take an entry level job at a local insurance company. This would allow me to save money to pay off my coming student loans and save up for my own apartment someday. As graduation drew nearer, however, I found that I couldn't bring myself to do it. I was seized by an urgent fear that I was embarking on someone else's life. I reminded myself that I still had a chance to begin the adventurous life I used to want. When would I ever get to travel, if not now? I was young, single, and childless with a bit of savings and no immediate financial obligations. I psyched myself up and decided to throw caution to the wind: I bought a one-way plane ticket to a foreign country, and made plans to leave the week after graduation.

The next few months were confusing to my friends and family. It had been years since I'd expressed a desire to travel, and seeing a usually even-keeled person throw sensible plans out the window can be disorienting. In contrast, I had never felt more alive. I floated on air waiting for the day I'd step on an airplane and be free. When asked what I would do for money and how I would communicate in a new country, I would smile brightly and chirp "I don't know!" to their dismay. I felt invincible. This feeling of empowerment carried me through the last months of my college career. It carried me through my loved one's tearful goodbyes, and it carried me *nearly* all the way through my international flight.

At the end of the flight, the pilot announced that we were making our final descent. I looked out the window eagerly, only to find that I was peering into an alien landscape. I couldn't make sense of the terrain or the sprawling city below me. My former teacher's words echoed through my head, augmented by my own fears. What if I truly didn't have what it took to enjoy a life of adventure outside of my comfort zone? How could I come creeping home with my tail tucked between my legs? I leaned back in my seat and closed my eyes, willing myself to stay calm. As the plane jolted down for a bumpy landing, I found a similar jolt of excitement in my stomach. I felt a wonderful surge of adrenaline as the plane bounced down the runway. We came to a stop and the cabin door opened. Passengers around me began to stand and rustle for their belongings as the smell of exotic spices wafted into the airplane. I took a long breath through my nose, reveling at the scent of adventures to come. I opened my eyes and smiled.

JB lives in Oakland, CA

Lost and Found

Speak up. Believe in yourself. Take risks.

~ Sheryl Sandberg

My childhood was greatly influenced by a culture in
which all social stratification is policed by age. In my
father's native language, there are many different forms
of address depending on both the gender and the age of
the person to whom one is speaking. This is so sharply
enforced that a peer exactly one day older than you
would be considered an "older" person and treated
accordingly. As the youngest girl in the family, you can
imagine that I spent a considerable amount of my
formative years keeping my opinions to myself.

This was especially frustrating when I could see a
coming train-wreck and no one would listen. I was a
teenager when my parents and a significantly older
sister decided to buy a home together. I cautioned both
parties against this as I could see that they had different
expectations of what co-ownership would mean. I
warned them that unless they got on the same page,
buying a piece of real estate together would lead to hard
feelings. No one paid any attention to my advice, and it
took several years for my sister and our parents to build
their relationship anew after a real estate-related near

estrangement. My take-away from that and countless similar interactions was to keep my mouth shut as my contribution wasn't valued.

I spent a year living in Mexico in my early twenties. I had traveled there to explore the country on the expectation that the weak peso would allow me to live off my savings, but I quickly ran out of money. Luckily, I managed to find a job teaching English, and it paid me well enough to keep a small room in the city and travel on holidays. One day my new friend Deb and I decided to go on a weekend trip. Deb had friends in a beachside town, and they offered to put us up in their place if we could get to their town. We had just enough funds to pay for a bus ride and buy a couple of days' worth of food, so we decided to go for it.

Friday morning we arrived at the bus station, and as my Spanish was much better than Deb's I just assumed I'd handle the transaction. Instead, she asked me for my half of the money so she could practice her Spanish by buying the tickets. I didn't really think this was a *great* idea but she was significantly older than me and about a thousand times more confident, so I capitulated. I hung back and congratulated her on what looked like a smooth conversation before we boarded our bus for the four-hour ride to the coast.

When we arrived at the place previously described to us as a "sleepy and small beach-side town" we were confronted with the sight of a huge oil tanker in dock. The entire city was teaming with people and traffic, which is much different from what we had been told to expect. We caught a taxi from the bus station and found that the taxi driver was completely unfamiliar with the address we gave him.

Puzzled, I asked Deb "Are you sure they gave you the correct name of the town? Manzanillo?"

"Yes!" she replied, self- assuredly, "I made sure to memorize the name of the town. It's 'La Manzanillo'. We're in the right place- let's get a better taxi driver."

"Wait a minute!" I started to get nervous now, "Was the name of the town 'Manzanill**o**' or '**La** Manzanill**a**?"

"What's the difference? Isn't that the same name?" Deb was starting to look nervous as well.

You can tell where this is going, can't you? We were supposed to meet Deb's friends in the sleepy town of La Manzanilla by 4pm at the school in which they taught. Instead, we found ourselves in the bustling city of Manzanillo at 3pm, 40 miles away along slow winding coastal roads into the next state. We only had enough money between the two of us for a couple of days' worth of street food and bus fare back home- there was no way we could even afford a hotel room to house us until the next bus left the following day. Faced with the enormity of our situation, Deb deflated.

I had a few minutes of panicked thoughts racing through my brain before I realized that Deb couldn't do anything to fix our situation. Even though I was used to keeping quiet and "following the leader" it was clear that I would need to navigate this situation for us. I took out all the cash I had in hand and asked Deb to do the same. Together, we separated out bus fare home and pooled the rest of our money together in a sad little pile. I took that money in hand and strode into the crowd of taxi drivers to haggle. They took one look at my American clothes and demanded a princely sum to make the trip. I told them I was not haggling, I was only offering all our earthly cash for this ride from Manzanillo to La Manzanilla, and I knew full well this was the fare they would charge a local. We carried on a 20-way shouting match with dramatic body language until one taxi owner was persuaded to make the trip. I grabbed Deb's hand and we shot into the backseat of the cab before he could change his mind.

As luck would have it, it began to rain on the drive so we

found ourselves hugging the mountainside and inching along with frequent stops to let a car pass on the opposite side. The taxi-driver spent the nearly two-hour trip bemoaning the fact that he agreed to our price and demanding more money than previously agreed. By the time we reached the town of La Manzanilla my throat was sore from all the arguing.

As soon as we approached the edge of town we paid the cab driver over the seat and ran from the car for fear that he'd keep the argument going. By the time Deb and I stopped running, we realized we were lost in a strange town, after dark. The rain had stopped but the ground was muddy and we kept sliding around as we walked. I could see Deb was starting to panic, so I strode out confidently and hurried her along as if I knew what I was doing. I decided we should walk in concentric circles from our location until we could find something or someone to help us along our way. The whole town had shut down for the weekend so our first 15 minutes were spent among closed business, dodging cat calls from young men who could tell we were lost. Eventually we passed by an outdoor taco stall where many of the townspeople had come for Friday night dinner. The smells of the taco stall were driving me crazy, so I wandered up to see the food and unexpectedly ran into our hosts!

In a stroke of luck for us, our hosts' stove had broken that day, so they happened to come along for a taco dinner right at the same time as we reached the stall. They took one look at our muddy, bedraggled selves and laughed, "Looks like you've had an adventure!" They treated us to dinner as we poured out our story. Afterward we danced to live music nearby, and then our hosts showed us to the ocean-facing rooftop where we'd sleep. I lay in my hammock and stared at the stars, feeling proud of myself.

I had learned a good lesson about trusting my instincts and taking charge of the situation if I'm the best person for the job. Our day could have been a disaster but through determination and a bit of luck everything had turned out fine. Our generous hosts agreed to lend us a bit of food money for the rest of the weekend and we would send them payment once we arrived back home. Deb and I were safe and fed, and we still had two days of beachside vacation ahead of us. I drifted off to sleep looking forward to the sunrise.

JB lives in Oakland, CA

A Courageous Journey

A Hero is an ordinary individual who finds the strength to persevere and endure in spite of overwhelming obstacles.

~ Christopher Reeve

I sat there on stage in front of all of my high school classmates and their families, speaking in a voice that was an octave or two above where it should have been, trying to keep my thoughts straight and heavily relying on the note cards in my hands. As I was giving my valedictorian speech, I scanned the faces of a rapt audience. I was about to give my speech, reflecting on past experiences and inspiring graduates to excel in the future. Trying to have them recognize the hero within themselves.

This was my first public appearance since a devastating car accident threw me into a severe coma nearly three months earlier. I was walking across the street and was hit by a car that was traveling at 50 miles per hour. Both of my legs were shattered, but the worst damage was to my brain after I flew through the air and my head crashed on the pavement.

When the Vice-Principal had told my parents that I was to give a speech at graduation and I tried to write something, my mind was blank. In the end, my dad helped me write a speech about courage, thankfulness, kindness, and how this was the start of the rest of your life.

For me, however, due to the after-effects of my severe coma, I was thinking and comprehending like a 12-year-old in an 18-year-old body.

The first thing I can remember in the hospital is day 15 after my accident and waking up in a room with a lot of people in it. Everyone was laughing and smiling, happy because this was the first day that I was really interacting with others. The phone next to the bed rang a couple of times, I answered it and talked nonsense into the receiver. I told one person that I was in a skiing accident and had broken both legs, but I'd be out soon. When the phone rang again, this time I proclaimed that I was in the hospital and I'd been shot, but I was getting better. What I was doing is called confabulation, which is making things up and believing they are true because there is no memory to say that it wasn't true. I really had no idea what was going on, and that's what I came up with. This day was the start of my long heroic journey back.

When the neurosurgeon spoke with my parents on the day I awoke from my coma, he told them that I should be able to take care of myself, but not to expect much more than that. He wanted to set the stage for my future life that was not to be filled with academic accomplishments, but hopefully I'd be able to live a life that was meaningful in other ways.

I'm glad I didn't know any of these poor predictions, because they may have made me think negatively. I was unable to recall many past memories and needed to start over to build for the future. Forge new frontiers, deal with issues as they arose, and work together as a part of a community network on a common goal to overcome barriers.

During my difficult college years, I had to teach myself how to learn again. After experiencing a traumatic brain injury, even though new information is presented to you, it doesn't sink in. So a few minutes after something had been presented, I couldn't even remember that it had been discussed. It was like a tape recording simply wasn't recording, and when I tried to recall the information, there was nothing there to recall. The only way I could get around this obstacle was to repeat, repeat and repeat, talk to my professors, beg for leniency, and try my hardest not to fail. That first semester I was taking microeconomics, macroeconomics, calculus and English, and somehow I managed to earn four low C's. Each semester slowly got a little better, and at least I didn't fail anything. I was determined to finish college, and I wasn't a star student but I did it!

Ever since I was a young, I had dreamed of developing myself into an international businessperson. I needed to expand my horizons outside of Western New York State and experience what the world had to offer. I needed to complete my college studies and go on to graduate school if I wanted to accomplish my goals. So I kept pushing and never gave up. In the end I earned one Bachelor's degree and two Master's degrees, and was then ready to explore the possibilities in this great world.

I moved to San Francisco after college, met the love of my life, and we raised three wonderful daughters together. Even with my severe brain trauma, I was able to have a successful career, with the final chapter being at the University of California. If at first you don't succeed, try a different route until you do.

A lot of what we have, we are born with. But our lives depend greatly upon what we do with which we are born. It's as if we each begin as a unique mound of lumber – each an unmatched mixture of redwood, oak and pine – with the sole responsibility of making the most of what we have to build the best life that we can. We do not start out as equals; our mounds are not and cannot be the same. But it is left to us to maximize ourselves, to learn how to use the tools and resources that we do have in order to produce a desired goal. We are not all equal in our intelligence and abilities, because we each have distinct purposes. We have been endowed with just the right amount of intelligence and ability in specific areas to fulfill that purpose, and it gives us a base to grow from there. Therefore, we do have an equal opportunity to grab a hold of our life and decide where to take it, even when it defies the odds of success.

Everyone has a story to tell and we each have our own strengths and weaknesses. Life is full of challenges and it is difficult to conquer obstacles unless you believe in yourself and your abilities. Most people can do more than they give themselves credit for, and it usually takes introspection and hard work to solve problems.

You are the Hero of your own story. Each of us has a unique journey, and none of us will ever be perfect. The successes and defeats of winning one battle and losing the next provide the incentive to keep moving and keep pushing. It's the journey toward them that makes life a challenge and what makes it great. It takes a lot of work, but the best things in life are often those that are earned. As Sophocles says – without labor, nothing prospers.

Keep Learning, keep growing, keep giving back. And be sure to recognize the hero within yourself.

Carol Lake lives in the Bay Area

Chapter 3
Recognizing the Hero Within

Finding Yourself

A Unifying Language

Music is the universal language of mankind.

~ Henry Wadsworth Longfellow

Her pink, sparkly skirt twirled as her partner gently guided her around the dance floor to the music of Hoagy Carmichael singing Stardust. Roseland restaurant, an Italian restaurant serving various Italian specialties in Buffalo, NY, also had a bar and was a popular stopping place for the local community. The patrons swayed to the gentle music played by the band, and this function of music and movement created a space where people could momentarily escape the rigors of daily life through the simple pleasure of dancing.

The band was called The Downbeat Trio, and consisted of a piano, saxophone and drums. The members of the band performed nightly to earn a few dollars and practice their craft. They were all recently out of high school, were not a part of the musical union and were amateur musicians who earned $1 per hour. They played for 4-5 hours three nights per week so that the restaurant and bar patrons could have a better experience while dining.

Vin was the pianist in the group, and his musical education commenced when he was 13 years old and his parents paid $2 a week for a guitar teacher to come to their house and teach him guitar. Their family finances were very tight, as Vin's dad was a baker and didn't make much money. There was always enough for them to eat, however, and the $2 a week for a guitar lesson was quite a treat. Taking formal guitar lessons provided Vin with a solid foundation in music theory, rhythm and finger dexterity. He took lessons for two years, and this served as a springboard when venturing into the world of piano.

Armed with nothing but passion, perseverance, and a relentless hunger for knowledge, Vin embarked on a voyage that relied on ingenuity and resourcefulness. He started playing the piano when he was 15, and he taught himself how to do this by using the guitar chords as his left hand, and the melody was played with his right hand. Playing the piano to Vin was like getting the protrusion of metal teeth in the machine's gear to properly fit into its counterpart so it could operate, with the chords and melody working in synergy to convey emotions and tell a story. If one doesn't dominate, beautiful melody and beautiful lyrics fit together to create a great song.

Vin grew up as an only child and he always wanted to make new friends because home was so quiet; it was pleasant but quiet. He was used to doing things alone, spent a lot of time with his own thoughts, then he worked on building close relationships with his friends. Everyone he met could be a potential new friend, and a friend may be waiting behind each stranger's face.

As he sat at the piano, Vin realized that playing the piano was not just about mastering the instrument or the musical notes, but it was also about building connections. Alone we can affect a few, but together we can change the world. Through self-discovery and introspection in the self-taught process, Vin gained a better understanding of himself and his place in the world. Music had grown to be an integral part of Vin's life, a steadfast companion. Music has the power to bring people together, forging bonds of friendship and solidarity, and uniting people from all walks of life.

Music is within all of us. Finding music within us is tapping within our innate ability to appreciate, create and connect on a deeply personal level. As Galileo Galilei states, "You cannot teach a man anything, you can only help him find it within himself."

Carol Lake lives in the Bay Area

My Friend Art

Art is not what you see, but what you make others see.

~ Edgar Degas

Art is my best friend. I've known her for a long time, ever since I was very little. She and I didn't meet by accident. In fact, she was forced into my life and, at first, I resented her. I resented the person that made me think of something on my own, something other than the "right" answer.

Art is the friend who introduced me to the world of creativity. We haven't always had the best relationship, but we've come a long way. People always tell me that she and I go perfectly together, that it's so amazing what we can do together, but it's not always as effortless as it may seem. It can be difficult spending hours on end with someone, even if you love them.

The special thing about Art and I is that she will always wait for me if I decide I need a break. She will always be there for me to come to when I realize I need her. She will be there, right where I left her, as soon as I hear my creative addiction calling.

In some ways I will always have a craving to paint the outside of a box rather than cowering inside of it, or to sketch my feelings out on paper rather than letting them stew inside of my head. Art is free, and Art is freeing. I pick up my pencil, my pen, my brush, my instrument of choice, and I create a version of myself on paper, different each time.

I need Art to survive just as much as my lungs need oxygen and my body needs nutrients. Art has introduced me to so many people who, today, I am so lucky to call some of my closest friends. She makes me happy and allows me to make other people happy.

Robin lives in San Diego, CA

Pancake Enthusiast

All you need is pancakes. Pancakes are all you need.

~ John Lenon

For some reason I've always had this unusual fascination with the faces restaurants make with fruit on their pancakes. I've come to realize that a pancake is as much a surface for art as is a canvas. The ingredients used to generate such a perfect consistency and flavor are only the beginning.

I am a self-proclaimed pancake enthusiast and I have been perfecting my Bisquick recipe for years. As it turns out, there is a recipe on the box that yields a deliciously standard pancake. Two cups mix, one cup milk, two eggs, and you're ready to griddle. If cooked correctly according to the instructions, the result is a fluffy, light, ordinary pancake. Sure, some may enjoy a simple, plain, fluffy pancake, but I strive to create pancakes that satisfy my curiosity as well as my stomach. How is it any fun to just follow the instructions put right in front of you? Let's get some cinnamon in there! I'm in a purple mood, red and blue food coloring can't hurt. Accidentally spill in too much salt? Feed them to your parents, they're obligated to say it's good (or just put some chocolate sauce on top to have a sweet and salty masterpiece, but it's your choice).

Now once you've got that pancake, made just to your liking, next comes the fun part. Feeling some Van Gogh? Take some Nutella and decorate your fluffy friend with some impressionistic strokes. Want a pal to keep you company as you devour your delicious dessert? Make your meal come to life with some strawberry ears, blueberry eyes, and syrup whiskers to create a companion that's as fluffy on the inside as it would be on the outside.

Finding food I like hasn't always been my strong suit. I'm about as picky an eater as it gets. Making cooking fun and eating a game has made me more willing to try new things and also encourage others to try what I make, despite my lack of cooking skills in areas other than pancake crafting.

Robin lives in San Diego, CA

Room to Grow

In every walk with nature one receives far more than he seeks.

~ John Muir

"They smashed Sandy!" my friend screamed as she inspected the bed. They probably just strolled by, casually plucked it off its roots and decided to play a recreational game of 'let's-see-who-can-throw-it-the-farthest'. I, on the other hand, have to stare at the scattered remnants of what was yesterday a beautiful watermelon, hand-grown by myself and my team, which we planned on eating after another day of hard work in our school garden. And yes, we did name a watermelon Sandy, after the Spanish word for watermelon, sandia.

Gardening isn't exactly 'cool' at my school; most people don't even know we have a garden. Though it's small in comparison to some of the other ones I've seen, I love it because my fellow eco-freaks and I made it from virtually nothing. It's become my home. Shoveling in the soil with the all-dreaded dirt under my fingernails, knowing that, in just a few short weeks, the seeds will be sprouting and blooming. I love being able to unearth the various fruits of my labor, to be quite literal, and donate them to local food banks and charities.

And I love learning about everything from the different fertilizers that the earth produces naturally to which cover crops to use depending on the levels of carbon and nitrogen in the soil. I even love the responsibility that comes with caring for a couple thousand seeds every season. It's more than just a hobby.

Still, many others feel differently. Besides those who steal our vegetables and vandalize our garden beds, some of my closest friends shove it off as lame, claiming I'm some sort of "hippie" or "tree-hugger". And yes, I have hugged a few trees in my day, but that's beside the point. I found my place working in our little garden, and I discovered a community of people that share my same interests and passions. Last year, for example, I was invited to a retreat for garden leaders in Northern California; I got to meet other students who talked about the enthusiasm and school pride that their gardens created, putting in school-wide composting and recycling systems, and some even had school farms! I was inspired.

Some people say my dreams are a little too big for such a small person, especially when it comes to the garden. You see, I have this master plan to make it not-so-little anymore. Our current garden is being torn down next year as collateral damage from our school remodel, but all I can see is opportunity.

We could get a bigger plot of land. Or a greenhouse. Or maybe even a cow or two if we're lucky. A couple of friends and I have already started plotting it out - though a more modest version than I anticipated - and we plan to present it to administration as part of our senior project later this year.

So yes, maybe I am a "hippie" or a "tree-hugger", but I know what I want. I want to do something that makes me feel the way I do when I garden. I want to be part of a close-knit community, with people who understand how much fresher garden-grown carrots taste as opposed to those store-bought, pre-packaged ones. I may not know exactly what direction that will take me in, but I know there's a world of options out there for me to explore. Somewhere out there is a plot of land just waiting for me to put a few garden beds on it. After all, I've had a little practice with that.

Sidney lives in Stanford, CA

Are You Smarter Than a 5th Grader?

In the end it's about the work, not an award you get for the work.

~ Linda Florentino

The curious eyes are still engraved in my mind. I recall the fearful expressions of the shy, the hollow thoughts of the ignorant, and the boastful moods of the arrogant. Fifth graders may be small, but they sure do have loud personalities. I remember pacing around the crowded cafeteria, memorizing the smell, feel, and rush of the moment. Nothing compares to the sweet smell of science in the morning. It was a pleasant day in April, and the children stirred in excitement, anticipating the start of the science fair. Awaiting my instructions as a judge, I stood patiently in the main hall.

I reminisce about the trembling hands of the scientists, and the shaky voices of those I judged. A young girl with glasses who simply couldn't speak because of fear – she had an interesting topic, and a lot of information, so I ended up giving her a good score report in the end. She reminded me of myself in a way because I always used to be so quiet and timid, especially when giving presentations. Maybe one day she will become more outgoing like I did. It's a shame too – the shy kids never really get much attention, especially at big events like science fairs. The superstars, the geniuses, and the outgoing kids always seem to get the spotlight. At the science fair, it's not always about the final presentation, however, but rather the thoroughness and creativity of the work. I remember the face of a boy who simply didn't care; about science, about the project, about anything. He stared at me, read his notecards in a monotone voice, and then I left. A lot of the students were like this too; I can only assume that their parents forced them to join Science Alliance, which is a shame. Science has always interested me.

I remember the last boy I judged that day. I wish I knew his name, because he taught me a lot about not only myself, but of the natural ways of people in the world. His fancy words, complete details, perfect poster board, and sculpted model of a rocket blew me away. He stood in front of me for five minutes, explaining the mechanisms of a rocket, and the physics of flight. It was as if he was teaching me. A fifth grader. Teaching a junior in high school. Concepts I had never even heard of before. I stood there, wide eyed and open mouthed as he explained his project in detail. I liked him not only because he was intelligent, but because he truly cared about the topic. I could tell he had really studied and prepared for his presentation, and I *knew* he had a passion for science. He actually wanted to be there, and I did too. I stood in front of the boy with a blank stare and an open mind, as I gave him a perfect score, and headed on my way.

The last time I saw the boy, he was crying. He was sobbing because he didn't get the award he wanted. Of course he had won first place. He really did blow away all of the judges. He had learned something new about physics. He had completed the project by *himself.* He was upset because he didn't win the sweepstakes prize. Of course there was another participant who found the cure to cancer, or figured out how to make a water powered car; so that student won the prize.

There may always be someone smarter than us, but that doesn't mean we shouldn't try. In the past few years, I've noticed that I continue to be surrounded by smarter and more intelligent people. It's scary and intimidating, and sometimes it feels like everyone is superior to you. Though this is true, I've learned that the only thing you can do is make the best of the situation. Instead of drowning and silencing yourself because you're afraid to be looked down upon, you should take it as an opportunity to learn more from those around you.

I sat curiously on the bleachers just watching the little fifth grader. My thoughts began to wander as I remembered all of those times when I wasn't perfect. When I didn't win everything.   When I wanted the greener grass on the other side of the fence. I just wanted to be the best.

What the boy didn't realize was that he had won. Not just a piece of gold plastic to place around his neck, but he had won. He had gained so many things from the experience, and that matters more than a ranking. I know at the time, though, it does seem like the world is crashing down around you. When you don't win it all, especially after working so hard, it's going to feel depressing. I haven't gotten what I've wanted a lot of times – it's the drawback to being a perfectionist. You have to take what you can get from each situation, though. If all you get from a fifth-grade science fair is a participation award and the knowledge you have gained, you should consider yourself lucky.

I always think of that boy whenever I don't get the grade I want, or I desire something someone else has. I don't care about them, because I have it all. It's all about making the best of what you're given. And now in every situation, whether it be good or bad, I win.

Seny lives in Castro Valley, CA

It's Good to Keep Your Humor

Even if you have a terminal disease, you don't have to sit down and mope. Enjoy life and challenge the illness that you have.

~ Nelson Mandela

You never really understand the toll a disease takes on a person until you learn their life story. You may read about the biological aspects of the disease in a college classroom, but to fully appreciate the complexity of human diseases, you must hear from those who are experiencing it firsthand.

I had the great opportunity of shadowing a neurologist in Illinois, and was able to interact with individuals suffering from a variety of neurodegenerative disorders. The doctor I shadowed was working with a team to carry out 12 clinical trials associated with helping individuals diagnosed with Multiple Sclerosis and Alzheimer's Disease. Reading the protocols was fascinating because I was witnessing cutting edge science – these drugs weren't FDA approved yet and were in the first stages of human trials.

When I first heard this, I was a bit scared to think that these patients were willing to try a drug that had only been proven effective on animals. After pondering this some more, I thought about the terror these patients must feel in knowing that they have an incurable neurodegenerative disorder. Though this is true, watching the patients explain their stories dramatically altered my view of how these neurodegenerative disorders affect everyday life.

I saw many patients while at the clinic, but a few stood out to me. One patient seemed angry with her Multiple Sclerosis diagnosis, and even went as far as to say she would shave off all of her hair just to be feeling better. Only at that moment did I begin to understand the hardships of the disease – the numbness, the lack of balance, the stiffness and pain, and the memory decline all seemed like I was surprised when a patient with the same worsening condition refused any treatment at all. In fact, I am quite appalled when people refuse any sort of treatment for a curable problem. Why would you want to be miserable for something that is so easily helped? One of the most interesting patients was one with many physical and mental complaints. Not only had she been seen by a variety of doctors, but none of the procedures had made her feel any better. Maybe some people will never be fully content with their current situation, and will always want more.

My favorite patient was the first patient I saw in the

clinic. Mike had come in to receive an infusion of a drug to help treat his Multiple Sclerosis. When I first met him, I felt nervous because I wasn't sure how to interact around patients with this disease. I watched him talk to the neurologist, and then he had a complete neurological screening. I immediately felt better when the patient exclaimed, "I'm a bit ticklish, sorry", as he pulled away while the doctor tested his reflexes. And I continued to laugh, when he asked me to make a bet of what I thought his blood pressure would be. Eventually the doctor told Mike to do ten laps around the building, and he knew this would be difficult because he had lost a lot of feeling in his right leg. Though, as he made every round, he would make sarcastic comments like, "I'm too old for this," or "I'll be there eventually, I hope." These comments made me think a lot. This man has such a great attitude even though he is constantly losing his ability to walk. If a man in this situation can still have a positive attitude, why can't I?

I began to think about the fragility of life and the fact that I am so lucky to live the life that I live. I imagined being told that I have a neurodegenerative disorder and will slowly lose motor function. Would I be angry that I was cursed with this fate? Would I have so much faith that I would refuse treatment and accept the idea that everything happens for a reason? Would I continuously seek treatment in hopes of one day living a better life?

Or would I accept my situation, look at it with humor, and make the best of it? I truly hope it would be the last one. Maybe in reality, it would be a mixture of all of the responses, but I think acceptance in this situation would be the only way to live a fulfilling life.

At the end of the day, I went home thinking about Mike. I didn't get a chance to say goodbye, or to say thank you. I think the worst part is the fact that I will never get to know how he ends up. Will the drug slow the progression of his Multiple Sclerosis? Will he be able to walk without a limp again? Maybe that's the beauty of research and medicine. Even if you never know the outcome, you can live in peace knowing you did all you could to help someone. It is possible I learned more at the Winter Shadow about myself and what it means to be a scientist than I did about treating the disorder. I love science because you can really make a difference in someone's life, and at the end of the day, that is what I want to do.

Seny lives in Castro Valley, CA

Chapter 4

Recognizing the Hero Within

Resilience

Courage Through Community

"Courage doesn't always roar. Sometimes courage is the quiet voice at the end of the day saying, 'I will try again tomorrow.'"

~ Mary Anne Radmacher, writer and artist

It was a Friday evening in July when I smashed my brain. I didn't mean to do it. No one ever does, I suppose. The next day I was supposed to drive to San Diego to launch my year as the elected president of a non-profit organization, an organization I loved. I had my PowerPoint ready, my notes all written out, and my hotel booked. It was time for a summer evening ride on my beloved horse, June, a perfect way to wrap that week before diving into this new adventure as a leader.

It was both warm and cool in the perfect way California can be in the summer. I threw my bareback pad onto June and led her to the mounting block. I swung my leg over her back just as she took a few quick steps forward. And then she took many more, much faster. It isn't unusual for horses to bolt - they are animals after all - but most of us who ride have experienced this and know how to react. You think quickly and take measures to slow the horse or change the direction and regain control. In this case I don't know if I did any of those things. I remember *thinking* about doing them but the very last thing I remember was sitting down and the swift momentum of her running under me.

And then the world stopped.

There was silence and nothing. So much nothing that I don't even remember it. It is a nothing absolutely lacking in sound, time, or sense.

The next few hours seemed simultaneously very quick and so very long. People held ice packs to my head while calling my husband. My husband took me to the ER where they made me track things with my eyes, take CT Scans, and lay in a hospital bed doing a lot of nothing. I do remember seeing my husband sitting next to my bed, with lots of worry on his face.

At the hospital the nurse told me I had a concussion and that I might feel dizzy for a few days but to go home and rest. As anyone with a traumatic brain injury can tell you, everyone experiences this differently; one brain injury is only one brain injury. Healing takes time and that time varies for each person.

Typically, a concussion or TBI is supposed to take eight weeks or fewer to heal and once you are past that timeframe, it becomes something that is sometimes called post-concussive syndrome. I learned this term as I spoke with my doctors at roughly the 10-week mark post injury. I learned that once you pass the initial eight weeks, there isn't any real way for them to tell you how long you will be in recovery. When that sunk in, I remember feeling the world fall away. I am not one to give up easily and I pushed for any therapy I could get approved through insurance. It turns out that it was mostly physical therapy and I immediately started doing vestibular physical therapy. I was tired of lying around, hoping I would get better, only to get up and not be able to walk straight. The physical therapy made a huge difference for me. I was asked to do simple things like walk down a hallway while tossing a tennis ball in the air. Sounds easy, right? Try doing it when your brain can't make sense of how the world is tilting.

I did therapy for four months before the doctor felt I was ready to jump back into my more active lifestyle. During this time, I was told to stay off my horse, which was the worst punishment for me.

The hardest part of recovery for me was not being able to do things for myself and feeling like my horse and dogs were suffering because I couldn't be as active as I had been with them before the accident. I felt useless and it was the loneliest time in my life. Each day, I was unable to do much more than wake up, do physical therapy, take a bath, read a few emails, and then sleep. I couldn't run my business, walk my dogs, ride my horse, wash dishes, walk downstairs without gripping the railing, or take a shower without feeling dizzy. And this went on for over a year before I found a TBI community.

Slowly I started to improve. I am not an incredibly patient person so I wasn't improving quickly enough, in my opinion, but according to doctors, I was doing really well. After about 18 months of this slow and lonely recovery, I finally found a local TBI survivors group. I have been attending those weekly meetings for the past year and it has made a significant impact on my outlook. The first few meetings were hard for me to get through without crying. I was finally surrounded by other people who fully understood what I was going through. I heard stories about people's injuries and strokes and while every story was unique, we all shared one thing in common: An empathy for others who struggled with simple tasks and an earnestness in our interest to lift one another up and encourage each other.

These new friends in my TBI survivors group were so honest about their struggles and grateful for each day and each lovely little thing. I started to see those things too. I started to take walks outside more often and started to marvel at the way the leaves filtered sunlight. I started to notice the busy little bodies of the honeybees and how the breeze, when it is that perfect temperature, just lifts the hairs on your arms and tickles your skin. Maybe I was just unwilling to notice these things before my accident, but after experiencing a traumatic brain injury that could have taken my life from me and the subsequent struggle that came with the recovery that followed, I am more willing to see that beauty each day.

I am not completely healed and I may never be the way I was before my accident. Every day that passes allows me to be more settled in that reality. I still have frustrating days and setbacks but I also celebrate smaller things that might have gone unnoticed before this experience. And I am riding my horse and doing my dog training again, which makes the world so much brighter. I am so grateful to the TBI community of which I am a part. Truly, I am more grateful for all of it.

Breanne Boyle lives in Orange County, CA

Speak Up

Nothing strengthens authority so much as silence.

~ Leonardo Da Vinci

I pace across the balance beam, each step a daring leap across the four-inch piece of wood. I stand still for a moment, thinking of the consequences of the dangerous trick I'm about to perform, and without turning back, I go for it. I arch my back, place my hands back on the beam, kick my pointy toes over my head, and land gracefully back on the beam. I've performed this trick millions of times, and as a competitive gymnast, practice is a necessity.

"No, Jenny, do it again," the criticizing voice of my coach rings in my ears. "You're not moving on until you make it perfect." I follow her orders, doing the trick numerous times, without thinking of the consequences. I mean, sure my back hurts every time I do this trick, but do I really need to tell the coaches? If I do, they'll make me sit out. They'll tell my parents, my teammates, and I'll be stuck on the sidelines. I don't belong there.

Two weeks later, I'm standing on the first place podium. Winning gives me a rush like nothing else in the world. I stare into the crowd of people, and I feel ecstatic because I know I've earned my reward – at a great cost though. My back pain is becoming unbearable. *No, don't give up,* I think to myself. I want to win, and a little pain isn't going to stop me from winning and doing the thing I love most.

Before I know it, I'm sitting at the spine specialist's office awaiting the news I dread most. I had to tell my parents of the pain. I just had to. First my parents, then my coaches, and now I'm sitting here, in the hospital. Sometimes I just take things too far to get what I want. But then again, doesn't everybody?

So I sit on the sidelines every day still, recalling the disappointing news from the spine specialist. "I'm sorry, but you have fractured your spine. You'll need to wear this back brace for a while." This isn't going to stop me though. I go to the gym every day, doing what I can, and telling them when I'm hurting.

Eight months later, I decided to go back to gymnastics, because my doctor said it should be okay. When I competed the next year, I promised that I would speak up. I became more outgoing, active, and used my fortitude to become a stronger person. It's okay to want to win, but it's not worth the pain. It's okay to tell others what I feel. It's okay to be *me.*

From this experience, I have learned to always have the courage to make a change, risk it all, and speak up for yourself. As one road ends, another will always begin. So embrace the chaos, and enjoy the ride.

Seny lives in Castro Valley, CA

Community

I always tell young girls, surround yourself with goodness. I learned early on how to get the haters out of my life.

~ Michelle Obama

I was leaving for my morning walk with my dog when I noticed a stranger sitting and smoking on my building's stoop. I live in a densely populated city, and it isn't altogether unusual for people without fixed addresses to pause their wandering for a smoke break on our steps. He greeted me politely, and I did the same. I didn't think much of it although I was surprised to see him still sitting there upon my return some minutes later. I nodded at him and continued up to my building door. As I took out my keys, I could hear him say something. My hearing isn't the best so I turned halfway around and asked "Pardon?"

"Can I have some of that ass?" He asked, leaning forward and leering at my rear end. He continued on crudely with other things he'd like to do to me and my body, but I couldn't really understand him over the loud ringing in my ears. I became aware of many things at once:

- A rush of shame as I remembered congratulating myself on how good my butt looked in these jeans this morning
- A second rush of shame for feeling that initial rush of shame because I hadn't actually done anything wrong
- The way this stranger was positioned only a few feet away from me, yet firmly between myself and the open street
- The cold metallic ring of keys in my hand all in a jumble as I had not yet set out to separate out my building key
- The fact that my neighbors closest to the building foyer (and therefore within best hearing range) were probably not home due to their weekday schedules
- The low odds of being able to get myself and my small dog into the building without harm if this stranger chose to rush at me right this second
- Guilt for assuming that someone would attack me just because he propositioned me crudely and didn't look to be sober
- Panic because I could very well be on the precipice of an attack

All of this washed over me in the instant before I opened my mouth and proceeded to turn the air blue. I hoped the force of my words would keep this stranger at bay long enough to pick out my key, jump in the door with my dog, and close the door behind me. Luckily it worked, although he peered in to track me as I walked through the front hall and up the building stairs.

Later, as I made to leave my apartment for work I noticed that the stranger was still sitting on the steps. Luckily I was at an angle to look out to the front stoop without being seen, and I noticed that he was now turned sideways, as to keep an eye on the comings and goings of the building's inhabitants. Deciding to be safe rather than sorry, I retreated back into the building and exited via the back stairs. I called my neighbors to give them a heads-up and also to ask them to see if they could get this guy to move along. Luckily, he was gone by the time I came home from work that night.

I posted about this incident on my Facebook page and I was struck by how many of my friends empathized with me. So many of us women have found ourselves in situations where we've got to ask ourselves if it would be better to fight or flee. Later, my dad heard of this through the grapevine and gave me some pretty well-meaning but useless advice on what to do in that situation. I can't blame him for being worried about his daughter, but frankly he's never had the experience of being harassed or threatened with assault by another human being. Worse still, my father tried to tell me that I should refrain from leaving the house when it's dark outside (conveniently ignoring the fact that this particular incident happened in broad daylight). I shut that line of conversation down pretty firmly as I'm a grown woman who exists outside of daylight hours. Leaving the house before dawn or after dusk isn't an invitation to be harmed! That sort of victim-blaming is unconscionable.

I've been threatened with violence by men too many times to count, which is to say just about as often as most women receive those types of threats. I'm very fortunate never to have experienced an actual sexual assault, but I don't kid myself that it's a result of anything other than pure dumb luck. I do take comfort in the knowledge that my female friends and I look out for each other. As soon as I was away from my building, I contacted a female neighbor who works from home and asked her to put a note up warning the other women to be careful with this guy on our stoop. She and another neighbor went outside together with their dogs to make sure the guy was gone. Another female friend, having read my Facebook post, offered to come meet me after work along with her husband, so that the three of us could walk home together just in case this guy was still hanging around.

I'm a short woman who lives alone. I don't kid myself that this incident will be the last time I will feel unsafe, followed by a cycle of guilt for possibly overreacting and anger for being put in that position in the first place. I don't have any idea of how we can quickly or easily change our culture in this regard. However, I do take comfort in being surrounded by caring friends who have been there and are ready to lend their presence to keep fellow women safe. We should all be so lucky.

JB lives in Oakland, CA

A Change in Perspective

The thing I always say to people is this: 'If you avoid failure, you also avoid success'.

~ Robert Kiyosaki

I love roller coasters! The tingle of fear as we slowly ascend up the track...followed by the rush of adrenaline as the coaster car drops into a free-fall...it's all amazing! I especially love roller coasters that have loops, but that wasn't always the case.

Until I was about nine years old, I was adamant that any roller coaster I rode could NOT include a loop. I couldn't explain it, but something about going upside down terrified me, even though I knew rationally that there were plenty of safety features in the way of individual straps and bars on these rides. I just couldn't bring myself to do it.

Then one day my family and I went to the county fair where we walked around taking in the sights all day. Toward the end of the visit, my parents said that my 15-year-old sister and I could each go on one ride. My sister and I wandered the fairway looking for a good one when we saw a roller coaster that existed on a loop. It didn't actually go anywhere; it just started at the bottom and then went straight up into a loop many times over at high speed. In the way of older sisters everywhere, she decided that BOTH of us should go on this ride together headless of my (numerous, shouted) objections.

My sister kept a firm grip on my collar as we stood in line, and when we got to the front I thought I'd found my salvation. The height requirements showed that I was just a shade too short for the ride. My hopes of an escape were dashed when my sister bum-rushed me past a very bored ride operator. Once on the roller coaster I realized we had a scary problem. The coaster didn't have any chest straps and instead depended on a lap bar in combination with centrifugal force to keep people in place. As if this wasn't horrifying enough, there was only one lap bar per car. That means that it fit my older sister perfectly, leaving a few inches between my own lap and the safety bar. I tried to yell to be taken off the ride, but others around me were already screaming with anticipatory excitement, so I wasn't heard. Before I knew it, we were off!

I'll say one thing for centrifugal force: it's strong as hell. I spent the first few loops screaming my head off but I stayed firmly in my seat and before I knew it I was actually enjoying being thrown upside down with every loop. My sister could tell when I started enjoying myself and I caught her smug teenage look. Luckily I was having too good a time to care.

Suddenly, I realized that we were losing speed on our loops. What was happening? Each time around, we were going a bit slower, which was exponentially scarier. Eventually, the ride stopped at the top of the loop, which left everyone hanging upside down for long seconds. To my horror, I found myself straining to keep myself pushed up against my seat, since the lap bar didn't even come close to keeping me in place. This time, my sister and I were both screaming in terror as she desperately clutched what she could reach of my shoulders. My legs were shaking with the effort of keeping myself in place, and just as I thought I would lose the battle and slip out of the car, the coaster started up again, this time doing loops in reverse. I was so relieved I turned the air blue at the top of my lungs.

Eventually the ride came to a stop and we stumbled off extremely grateful to have made it out alive. We rushed over to our parents, expecting them to be beside themselves with worry. We were shocked to find them calmly waiting, and they were bewildered by our excitable state. We came to realize that what seemed to us like a slow-motion near-death experience from inside the ride looked exactly the same as a relatively safe high speed loop coaster from the ground. Our parents assured us that I never looked to have been in danger; what seemed like a gaping hole between my stomach and the shared lap bar was actually just a few inches that I would never have been able to slip through.

That was the day that I learned the value in examining a situation from different perspectives before making any decisions. Applied broadly, it's been an indispensable skill in both my personal life and my professional career. I'd like to think it's also helped me become a more thoughtful and deliberate person than I'd be otherwise.

Another nice consequence of that county fair experience is that I was never again afraid of highly regulated theme park roller coasters again, regardless of the number of loops involved. Bring it on!

JB lives in Oakland, CA

Overcoming the Loss of a Friend

The connections we make in the course of a life - maybe that's what heaven is.

~ Fred Rogers

I peered around the quiet dorm room on my first day of college with innocent eyes and blatant curiosity. I wanted to talk to someone – anyone really, I just wanted a friend in this new place that I would call my home for the next four years. To me, college seemed scary – you'd hear stories that this was the greatest time of your life, that this was the time you'd meet your best friends, and the chance to really become who you are.

"Oh hello there, are you Jenny?" A friendly voice from the room next door beckons me. I peer into his room, and the first thing I notice are the four bikes he has laying around – one of them is a tandem. "I'm Mark, your HA, it's nice to meet you! If you need anything, I'll be right next door." That's what I'll remember the most about Mark. He was always there – for everyone really. Whenever you needed him, he was just a text, a knock, or a holler away.

Not long after he graduated that same year, Mark was killed in a deadly biking accident. Nobody believed it. I know I didn't. I remember being on the phone with my best friend from college, and we were bawling our eyes out. How could Mark be gone? He had just finished his thesis, graduated with a degree in chemistry, and was on his way to becoming a real adult, or as he liked to call it, "adulting". (Things like living by yourself in Portland, getting a new library card, etc). The loss of a friend, especially someone like Mark, just seemed impossible, improbable, and unfair.

And that's when the reality of the situation hit me. Death is not a game, and it doesn't really feel real until you lose someone you care about. I learned that you're going to have regrets. You're going to want to see him again. You're going to want to change the past – you may even begin to wonder if you could have prevented the tragedy. You'll remember the last time you saw him. He did look pretty spectacular walking down the red carpet on graduation day in his long black robe and green hair. You'll remember how hard he struggled near the end. But most of all, you may not believe it. You'll think, "No, not Mark", and may even go as far as to say that someone else should have died. But it's all just so unfamiliar. And it still doesn't feel real.

The death of Mark was one of the biggest tragedies I've had to face in my life. The flashbacks, the smiles, and the laughter always seem to be the biggest struggle. I remember one time he was trying to tutor me for my chemistry final, but he actually fell asleep in the middle of a sentence – he was that exhausted from working, and still was willing to help me out. "Mark, you should really get some sleep!" I said, and he went to take a nap. I also think it's funny how every time my friends and I had a problem with anything we would think, "Well, let's just go ask Mark". (For bike help, help setting up projectors in the common room, help with chemistry homework, help with friend drama, etc). He was always the first person that came to my mind.

At the end of the year, only a week before he died, I slipped a letter under his door telling him how much he had helped me my freshman year of college. He was a role model for everyone – he was a pro fire spinner, bike enthusiast, chemistry whiz, and even had an article about him written in the Reed magazine entitled, "What it means to be a Reedie." Overall, I just miss him. Everyone who knew him does.

Since he passed away, I have tried to do the things he enjoyed doing. I joined the fire spinning club, and currently am trying to become a master at poi. (Spinning fire balls). I try to help others as much as possible, and think of him every time I get stuck on a chemistry problem. I hope I can be as generous as he was one day. And I hope the best for Mark as well, wherever he may be. That's the most important thing I learned from his passing. Maybe he can be where I want him to be. Where I know he would want to be. And where is that? Riding a bike on a beach somewhere, maybe. When I imagine him there, I start to feel a little better. Just seeing him smile again is enough to get me through even the hardest of days sometimes.

Seny lives in Castro Valley, CA

Extending a Helping Hand

It's a small thing to help one animal, but to that one animal it's a big thing.

~ Gene Baur

Working in an animal hospital taught me the importance of patience. The healing process for injured animals can take many weeks, and being a part of the recovery process made me feel like I made a difference. These animals needed me, and in a way I needed them. While I was helping them improve from their injuries, they were bringing perspective into my life. There were big birds, small ones too, and watching them grow gave me a sense of purpose.

My favorite birds were the scrub jays. Something about the way they sat in their little nests made me laugh all the time. To feed the little birds, we would make a mixture of kibble mix, calcium and other essential nutrients, and blend it into a soupy liquid. My favorite part was feeding the baby birds, because they would open their mouths wide for me, and they were always so satisfied after I gave them a syringe full of food. Sometimes they would spit it up though, and I felt bad every time.

On my first day, we walked into a back room full of snakes and red-tailed hawks, which they called the Behind the Scenes Room. This room consisted of a one-way mirror that was accessible to the public, so they could watch us feed the animals. Every day at around noon we would also give a presentation on a specific animal, and the little kids would ask questions. This was a great part of the wildlife hospital experience, because I could teach what I knew to the public. Some of the questions from the little kids were great too. They always wanted to know how big the bird would get, or how long it would live, and when we could take it back to the wild. The answers were usually the same because I always presented the scrub jays – they live for around nine years, and their feathers eventually become thicker when they are adults. The birds were usually in the hospital for around two weeks before they were released back where they were found.

In the back room, they also had a lot of crows. What I didn't know about crows is that they are really intelligent, and therefore it makes them difficult to feed. If they are particularly stubborn, you have to forcefully open their mouths and shove the syringe full of food down their throat. Many times this process was accompanied by a bird spitting up all over you or a bird that escaped from your arms that you had to chase down. This happened a lot actually – I learned that when a bird escapes, you should turn the lights out because it calms them down.

One day in the hospital, we had an intake of a mother opossum who had been hit by a car. They raced the mom in, and I remember seeing all the blood and the limp body of the mother. Before I knew it, they were opening her up and pulling out the baby opossums – 1..2..5.. 8 baby opossums! They were so small, and I remember holding them in my hands and thinking about how small they were. I guess it was weird to think that something so small eventually grows into such a huge and feared animal.

I loved squirrel intakes too. You could hold the baby squirrels in the palm of your hand, and they would crawl all over you. Of course you had to hold them with gloves, because their claws really hurt! We would mark squirrels with a stripe of marker on their tail, and when we tried to weigh them, they would make it so difficult. Such squirmy animals. We got deer and eagles and red tailed hawks and crows and hundreds of birds. We got to watch them grow and heal, and eventually we released them back into the wild. Some of the animals didn't make it though. That was the hardest part of the whole experience. You would put so much effort and time into an animal, and it wouldn't respond to medication or it would stop eating. And all you wanted was for it to get better. We had a deer who had a seizure, a hummingbird that stopped breathing, and many animals that were just losing too much weight. It was really frustrating, and when they would pass away, you felt like you failed. All I wanted was for them to thrive.

My time in the animal hospital taught me the importance of helping others. Whether they're birds, or people – helping someone in need always makes you feel better. Overall, the animal hospital taught me that I could really make a difference.

Flash forward and I'm suddenly in my junior year at college on a regular Wednesday. I was walking past one of the lecture halls, when I saw a group of students hovering around what appeared to be something on the ground. My curious self walked over to the group and stood peering down at the little bird on the floor. It had hit a window, and it was stunned and terrified.

"I'm not sure how to help it," one of the freshmen stated. "Maybe we should move it to the edge of the path so nobody steps on it?"

"Here, I worked in an animal hospital, I can take it back to my room and try to help it." I said.

Before I knew it, I was running across campus with an injured bird in my hand. I didn't want it to fly away, and at the same time I was afraid I would crush it. I got stares from everyone as I jogged to my room, and when I saw a few friends I held the bird out and said, "I'm helping a bird". They gave me weird looks, but dammit I was going to help this bird.

I found a container in my room, put some paper towel on the bottom of it, and ran to class. I didn't want to be late. Later that day when I went back to my room, I looked back into the container. The bird was gone. Oh no, I thought to myself. I frantically searched my room and found the bird crouched in a corner. It seemed to be doing okay. I could've opened the window and let it fly out, but I wasn't going to let it go without getting a picture with it first.

I chased the bird around my room for around 10 minutes. I'm glad nobody saw it because I would've looked ridiculous. When I finally caught it, I took a selfie, said goodbye and let it go. I'm glad it was feeling better, and I hope the warm room allowed the bird to snap out of its shocked state. That was the day I saved a bird. I wouldn't have been able to do it without my prior experience, and I felt good.

I felt great for the rest of the day. I had truly made a difference, and though the bird couldn't say thank you, I felt like I had done something. Next time I'm feeling down, I should try to make a difference. Help a friend, help an animal, help anyone really. Why not make someone's life better? Why not bring a smile to one's face? I live for those moments. A smile from a friend, a happy chirp from the bird – it's these little moments that make us feel like we can change the world.

Seny lives in Castro Valley, CA

Man's Best Friend

A dog is the only thing on earth that loves you more than it loves itself.

~ Josh Billings

In trying to determine what makes people happy – what are the basics behind why people do what they do in life – I created an informal survey of friends, colleagues and family, asking that very question. The responses I received were a little varied but most had the same underlying component – people like to help others. Three common responses I received were: helping another human being do something better, taking care of ourselves so that we can help others, or taking care of an animal in need. People like to share themselves with others who may not be as fortunate.

Many families have pets as a part of their everyday life. Owning a dog can add a new purpose to your life. Dogs can be the perfect companion if trained properly, are very loyal, do not judge you, and love you unconditionally. When you have a dog you are never really alone. Caring for a dog makes you feel like you are making a difference, and it adds another dimension to your life.

I decided to delve more deeply into why so many people are involved with helping an animal in need. I met up with an old friend, Linda, whom I hadn't seen in a long time and who was deeply involved in dog rescue missions. This was new to me, so I explored what she was doing so that I could understand how her efforts gave her life that extra meaning.

In 2011 Linda found out about a few friends who were starting a dog rescue effort and she decided to become involved. She started out by bathing the dogs upon arrival at the shelter, and from there she began traveling on the rescue missions. After a while she became involved in almost every aspect of the process, and is now the Manager, Treasurer and Intake Coordinator for the organization.

Furever Friends Dog Rescue of Western New York, Inc. is a 501©(3) non-profit organization incorporated in 2012, that rescues unwanted dogs and puppies from puppy mills, as well as creating awareness of the plight of puppy dog mill dogs. Prior to becoming involved with Furever Friends, Linda was often hesitant to become involved with animals in need, out of fear of the unknown. She had never entered an animal shelter, feeling as though she would be upset by what she saw.

Furever Friends travels to the Amish puppy mills in Ohio and rescues some of these breeder dogs, then takes them to a vet to be vaccinated and treated for any other medical needs they may have. The rescue team then brings them back and places them with dog foster families so that they can be cared for in a loving way and made ready to be adopted. On average, the dogs stay with the foster family for 4 to 6 weeks.

As background behind what happens in puppy breeding, many breeder dogs spend the first part of their lives confined to a puppy mill and treated like livestock. The dogs are confined to cages in puppy mills for the sole purpose of breeding to produce purebred pups that are sold to pet stores, and can be sold at a large price. The conditions in which the mothers are kept while producing their litters, however, is inhumane and often leaves the mothers ill with disease and sometimes near death.

Breeder dogs are released for a variety of reasons - the most common reason is that the female dogs at 5-7 years old are "used up" for breeding purposes. The females are forced to breed each time they are in heat, which amounts to twice per year for most.   After some time, their bodies simply can no longer produce puppies and many of these gals are very, very sick upon rescue.

The impact that becoming involved with Furever Friends had on Linda was striking – she was able to make a difference in the life of a dog who was being mistreated, and was able to have a direct impact on helping make things better. Linda gradually began to feel more at ease around mistreated animals. She now looks at the bigger picture, has seen how changing the life of one dog can make a difference, and also has gained more knowledge regarding the difference between reputable dog breeding, and breeding strictly for profit with no thought of the animal's well-being. As Linda took on more and more jobs within the organization, she gained more confidence in her abilities, which was something she had been lacking.

Puppy mill rescues require an abundance of love and patience in order to get the dog ready to be placed with a loving family. All potential fosters and adopters must complete an application, listing references, and they also must also undergo a home inspection to determine whether or not the dog would be placed in a safe environment. It's with this careful and deliberate effort that we can be sure these animals will now be a part of a loving and stable family.

This story started out as a simple meeting with an old friend to catch up and turned into a much larger focus of how people extend themselves to do what makes them happy – by helping another living being.

Carol Lake lives in the Bay Area

Chapter 5

Recognizing the Hero Within

Giving

Willingness to Give

Great opportunities to help others seldom come, but small ones surround us every day.

~ Sally Koch

I felt a hard and fast-moving object strike me and throw me high up in the air, and I heard a loud breaking noise in my legs. Volts of electricity seemed to vibrate throughout my body. My body then spun out of control and I crashed to the ground. Excruciating pain shot through my head. Am I unconscious? Impossible. Why can't I wake up? Why can't I move?

The witnesses said I flew 80 feet in the air and crashed down on the pavement. My body was lifeless, blood was oozing from my legs, and I was struggling to stay alive. It was fortunate that I was close to a major hospital or I could have died on the spot.

After being rushed to the emergency room, they could see I had two broken legs – one badly shattered – a broken pelvis, a fractured skull, and I was in a coma. My coma was severe, meaning that I could remain comatose forever or I could die.

My first few days in intensive care were complex, difficult and full of hope and prayers from those who were wishing for me to survive. My neurosurgeon visited me daily to measure the status of my coma, to see if I was getting any better. My brain was very swollen and was pressing on the confines of my skull. If this went on much longer, irreparable damage would be done to my brain. They may have to drill burr holes in my skull to relieve the pressure so that I did not develop permanent brain damage, but it had not been necessary so far. After 10 days I had emerged enough from my coma to be moved to a regular hospital room, however the first day I can remember is day 15.

I was in the hospital for two months, with my left leg in traction. It had been shattered and rods were put in to hold my bones together so they could heal. The funny part is, I didn't hurt at all. My doctor kept asking me if I wanted any pain medicine, but I said no, I don't hurt. It may have been the after-effects of my coma that kept me pain free, or the constant care and attention that helped me stay so comfortable.

My hospital stay was very positive. Everyone was giving back, giving their all. One of my night nurses took special interest in my well-being and monitored me closely; my roommate for four weeks was a high-priced escort who reported to my parents each evening on the events of my day; the Vice-Principal of my high school came to visit often and asked my parents how he could help. People, even those my family didn't know well, offered help simply because they could. The nightmare that had started this story had dissipated and turned into a reality of healing and re-building.

The real pain, however, started when I had to learn to walk again and comprehend what was going on in the outside world. The journey back was long and demanding, and this was the start of the formation of the new me. I took the positive feelings that had been given to me and used them as a base for my fight.

Trouble often brings out the best in people. It forces us to rally our resources and put our best foot forward. It's those of us who are able to get through difficult times without losing our faith that life can get better again if we just keep on trying - we are the true winners. Not because we've never experienced difficulties or encountered failures, but because we pressed on towards our goals, knowing that we would rise again should we fall. We have the power within us to use disasters to become stronger and grow in character, and not become bitter.

While I had moments when I thought of myself as a victim, I drew from my inner strength that told me I was not. If I had not, that would simply imply defeat and giving up would have been too easy. I have learned why my memory is bad and why some other things after my coma are the way that they are. Because I was not aware of these likely constraints, I did not have the emotional barriers to add to the physical ones that were making my fight challenging enough. I expected a full recovery, so I demanded it and earned it and made my dream real.

This trauma helped me become who I am today – kind, helpful, supportive, cheering for the underdog and wanting to help others. This new me was developed over a lifetime but started when my life almost ended; I felt the love and support from others during this time and wanted to continue to be a part of it. Even though it was a horrible thing that happened, I enveloped all of the love and support that was being given and it became a part of me.

I may not have consciously experienced all the positive wishes when I was in my coma, but I know they played a part in my ability to finish the job. I was able to graduate from college and graduate school, and the whole spirit of everyone giving was the base that started my recovery. Now I want to pay it back and helpothers as well, to work with other traumatic brain injury survivors and help them on their way in recovery. The fact is that in the end, the giver becomes a receiver too – a receiver of gratitude and of warming self-satisfaction for having helped.

All it takes is a willingness to give.

Carol Lake lives in the Bay Area

With Grit and Grace: Rebuilding after amnesia and brain trauma

Happiness is not something readymade. It comes from your own actions.

~ Dalai Lama

In May of 2000, a speedster ran a stop sign, hit me, my car rolled and they told me it took the Jaws of Life to get me out of that car. And I don't remember anything. I had suffered a traumatic brain injury (TBI), which left me with retrograde and anterograde amnesia. My past was totally gone.

My first memory was that I was in a human body, because I didn't even know that I had to deal with being human. Can you imagine how your day can become so complicated when micro-decisions are made to fulfill even the simplest tasks? Do I wet the toothbrush first or do I put the toothpaste on the bristles first? How many times a day do I brush my teeth? Most people are on auto-pilot as they complete their normal routines, but I had to create some kind of order to have everything make sense. Inhaling, exhaling, even breathing required me to think about what I was doing. I was thrown into a new world, one which I needed to figure out.

Why did I decide to have a "Happiness Project?" Because I noticed when you sit in the doctor's office and look at all the outdated magazines, there's a lot of articles on being happy. I then embarked on a journey to figure out what my happiness was. People have different versions of happiness, and I needed to find it for myself. My past memories had been erased because of my amnesia. It was fine that I didn't remember the accident itself, but everything else was gone too. I had a clean slate to make it up as I went.

What was my new happy? I didn't know, and it was complex enough to consider what kind of human being I was going to be. I saw an awful lot of different people around, so I thought that I needed to decide what characteristics I wanted to adopt. I thought that a lot of people like a happy person, so that's what I decided to become. I was learning that you have a choice, you could wake up each day and look for the good, or you could say poor, sad me. I decided to find the happy, the good, the kind.

Each day, we have a choice to feel and do good within ourselves and in the community. Either it's going to come from inside yourself, or if not, something like the sunshine making today a beautiful day is positive. If I was feeling down in the dumps, I would take a walk and say "hi" to people. It feels good to make others smile.

When I looked at my resume from before my accident, my first thought was – who is that? Before my accident I ran an accounting consulting company, but now I couldn't work with numbers so that wouldn't work anymore. I started volunteering at our local hospital, and I was able to experience a family having their own baby. I observed the happiness, joy and wonder of creating a new person. Oh, that's what it's like to have a baby! I didn't remember giving birth to my own children. I also didn't remember what it was like to go to college, and I had earned a number of degrees prior to my accident. I decided to go back to school and experience what it was like to be in school; I had to focus on things differently now. I had to create a new me and find ways to contribute to society and help others.

I was disappointed, in a lot of pain, and there was going to be more pain if I wanted to go out in the world. The pain went from being physical pain to emotional pain, because everyone was focusing on the negative side of my injuries. I wanted to find distractions and ways to give back to others.

I had started to participate in some head injury recovery meetings, and I found that there were a lot of people who didn't know how to get themselves into the next phase, or find resources for additional help. As I started talking to people, I discovered that many of these resources were not helpful for me.

I could have taken a negative attitude about that because I needed to find what would help me! So I started sharing these things that were not useful for me to others in my recovery group. Some others took that advice and it helped them – and guess what? That made me happy. It was a step outside of the darkness that I had fallen into; I was finding ways to help someone else.

I was earning my graduate degree with Peter Drucker at the Claremont Graduate University, and he saw all the resources I was uncovering for TBI survivors. I had researched my own recovery, working with doctors and therapists at local hospitals. Peter Drucker encouraged me to share my growing network of resources by forming a support group and website. I will always hold what Peter advised, "if no one else has put resources like this together in one place, you may have to". This guided me to create **Bridging the Gap connecting traumatic brain injury survivors** (www.tbibridge.org), and this is a robust online lifeline and resource connector for TBI survivors and their caregivers.

We all realize there's not one particular way to do it, but there has to be some way for each person to get outside themselves and outside of looking at things in just one way. If we look at whatever the problem is and try some different things, we'll find it. We take all the little bits and pieces of things that are going on, put them together, and this is how you find your happy.

Getting into something different, and we should ask for help if we need it, might make us start feeling a little better about ourselves and start feeling like we have more to offer. Write down the things you do well, and maybe sending someone a thank you note in verse would make their day. Practicing Random Acts of Kindness and giving someone a smile is another way to broaden yourself and be appreciative. There are so many things you can do to help someone in return and often people don't realize it. We are all here to help and support each other. As Winston Churchill said, "attitude is everything."

When Peter Drucker was asked what he wanted to be remembered for, he said being a great listener and a great observer. Watch, listen, then contribute if necessary. I met people who were great listeners and great observers, and they were the ones people gravitated toward. We can be purposeful in letting a little happiness into someone else's life and it will bring happiness into our own life.

Presented by Celeste Palmer of Bridging the Gap in Claremont, CA

Paying it Forward

The unselfish effort to bring cheer to others will be the beginning of a happier life for ourselves.

~ Helen Keller

Did you ever think, *what are people going to remember about me once I'm gone*? Many of us ponder that thought, and it's good to reflect on the memories we create and how our impact on others will be remembered.

Jane is a good example of embracing kindness and generosity to uplift those around her. The most important part about Jane's history is how she put it all together; the education, love for dance, perseverance, and desire to help someone else realize their dreams.

Jane was an Executive Assistant at a University for many years, and she spent her time ensuring that the organization functioned smoothly. Her selfless contributions helped build community, and her kindness was always well appreciated. There's a lot behind how she developed into her present self, and one kind donor started this positive momentum.

Jane's varied interests have taken her on many paths throughout her life. Jane is the youngest of four children, and her family's modest income didn't allow for extra frills such as dance lessons. Her mother used to work in a laundry, and she would talk about how her young daughter Jane really wanted to take dance lessons, but they really couldn't afford it. Jane would come visit her mom at the laundry occasionally, and Jane's spirited enthusiasm would entertain the other workers.

One day when Jane was 7, her parents got a call from the local Ballet School. An anonymous donor, the director said, wanted to pay for young Jane's ballet lessons. This gift was for 5 years of lessons, and this is how Jane's dance career began.

Jane later learned that the anonymous donor was a woman who worked alongside Jane's mom in the laundry department of the local Memorial Hospital. Her name was Mrs. Smith, and she and her husband raised Arabian horses and did not have any children of their own. Jane only had one conversation with the woman, and she told Jane, "I can spot talent in horses, and also in children." Mrs. Smith wanted to encourage that spark she saw in Jane's personality, and this was the start of a long dance career.

Jane studied ballet until she went to college, and even joined a professional dance company at 16 while still in high school. Jane was the first in her family to attend college, where she focused on dance while taking courses in things like French and art history   "you know", she adds with a touch of humor, "useful, career-type stuff". She paid for her own undergraduate education at a local liberal arts college and broadened her dance to include modern dance and other types of dance.

Jane's liberal arts education continued with studies at UC Davis, funded by a grant given by the Future Farmers of America. A few years later, severance pay from a layoff in the private sector enabled her to complete an MFA in Choreography at University of California. Jane persevered toward doing what she really wanted to do, and she always "found a way to make it happen."

To Jane, "arts are important – seeing a work of beauty. Dance, theater, music, they move me, they speak to me." Doing what you love, but also being practical, are keys to Jane's success. Throughout Jane's career, she has been in various administrative roles, but usually had a job that was flexible enough to pursue her art. When she got a gig to go to New York, she had to stop everything in California and catch up later. Jane was always sure to have a day job, though, and she made enough money to support herself and her art.

Years ago when the anonymous donor, Mrs. Smith, gave Jane the 5 years scholarship for dance lessons, she was paying it forward because she saw talent in young Jane, but also because an anonymous benefactor had paid for

Mrs. Smith's piano lessons when she was a child. So Mrs. Smith was now completing the circle and paying it forward for someone else.

Starting when Jane was on the board of a dance center in Berkeley, she contributed money to fund scholarships for up-and-coming students. Jane did this because she "knew what it felt like to really want to dance but not have enough money to do so." So Jane was now paying it forward to a new generation of dancers.

The key lesson we can take away from this is to never give up. If there's something you love to do, even if it's not a great income-generator, work toward finding a way to make it happen. If you can expand on something you enjoy and are good at, it could benefit others as well.

Carol Lake lives in the Bay Area

Take Care

We make a living by what we get; we make a life by what we give.

~ Winston Churchill

The walls of the library are adorned with a beautiful assortment of books, each one a gateway to increased knowledge. The blues, greens, ochre and other varied colors create a vibrant display that catches the eye of anyone passing by. These books are more than just paper and ink, but are a collection of stories and dreams waiting to be explored.

In a world busy with activity and responsibility, it's easy to overlook the quiet heroes among us - the caregivers who selflessly take care of the needs of our elderly loved ones and are their companions to overcome day-to-day challenges. Reading about diverse perspectives and emotions enhances the understanding of varied life experiences. Being an avid reader is helpful when faced with the task of caring for elderly relatives, as it helps with empathy, connection and understanding someone else's struggles. Combining the joys of reading with the responsibilities of caregiving can feed both the mind and heart.

The cycle of taking care of others and being cared for is a normal part of life, and it reflects how people in society are interconnected and how we rely on each other. My father is 95 years old, and has cared for aged relatives more than most. After dad retired, he took care of five elderly relatives who had no one else to care for them, and this allowed them to live independently into their later years. It began with his mother and aunt, and three others followed over a 20-year time period. It wasn't a chore for my dad to do this, it was just something that needed to be done.

Cousin Rosie was the relative my dad cared for the longest, and he did this for 20 years until she died when she was 92. Rosie was born before the Great Depression and witnessed families losing everything as financial systems collapsed, banks failed and businesses went bankrupt. This is one of the reasons Rosie didn't trust putting her money into the banking system, and instead used to keep her savings tucked away in little cubby holes around the house. Many of that generation felt the same way about banks; it was risky to keep so much cash around the house, but that was Rosie's way of feeling in control of her finances.

Helping these elderly relatives was often a challenging job for my dad, and he handled this with grace and compassion. Older people don't like change; they are used to things being a certain way and resist any deviation from the norm. Dad's main goal was to help them live independently for as long as they could so they could stay in their comfort zone. He made them feel like they were not alone, and made sure they lived safely so they didn't hurt themselves. Dad's philosophy is – caregiving is caregiving, not domineering another person. Help the elderly person stay upbeat, have them try to think good thoughts rather than bad ones, and make them laugh to help them overcome any negative thoughts they might have.

The act of giving without expecting anything in return is a selfless act that embraces the interconnectedness of people and the need to take care of one another. Caregiving is not only good for the receiver, it is also good for the person providing the care. My dad's caregiver duties helped him better understand what it was like to get to an advanced stage in life. This process also helped him feel positive about himself and gave a greater meaning and purpose to his life.

Now that my dad is of advanced age himself, it's time to reverse the roles and have him be the receiver rather than the giver of care. My brother Paul has stepped up to provide companionship to my dad and help him with day-to-day activities he can't do himself. This is completing the giving circle and allowing my brother to continue the ripple effect of positivity and generosity. As Helen Keller states, "We are never really happy until we try to brighten the lives of others."

Carol Lake lives in the Bay Area

Chapter 6

Recognizing the Hero Within

Life Lessons

Beginning at the End

Every failure is a step to success.

~ William Whewell

Mitch Albom once wrote, "All endings are also beginnings, we just don't know it at the time." Many of the pieces of wisdom I've gained throughout high school seem to have been retained as specific quotes, and I will be giving you some of my favorites today. For me, high school was a constant battle – fighting for grades, friends, attention, and mostly acceptance. Though this is true, the struggles of high school will soon be ending. It's up to us to rewrite the rest of our story, and hopefully conquer the battles to come.

Today, I'm here to tell you the most important lesson that I've learned throughout my life. Don't lose your inner child as you try to succeed. Look at stressful situations with simple eyes, and just maybe you'll find a moment of peace in this complex world. I've found moments of joy in high school by: skipping through the halls, laughing a lot, making car noises as I drive my car, playing board games, singing Disney songs as loud as I can, and being weird to make other people laugh. All these activities are juvenile and may be looked down upon, but I feel content every time I act like a child with my friends.

Calvin once said to Hobbes after a long day at school, "Let's go exploring," and throughout my life, I have found that sometimes when I'm stressed with school, homework, or even my family, an adventure is all I need to free myself from life's challenges. So don't lose yourself in the battle of finding your purpose in life – embrace your inner child, be rebellious, and live a little!

Children have to grow up eventually though, and will be faced with tough choices. Robert Frost once wrote, "Two roads diverged in a wood and I – I took the one less traveled by, and that has made all the difference." My advice to you all is that you take the road that is right for you, and stick up for your decisions. In this way only will you end up learning the most about yourself, and growing from your experiences.

I was in gymnastics for eight years, then did acrobatic gymnastics for two before I finally decided that wasn't my path. I stood up for myself because I had been hurt in the past, and when the coach kept telling me that everything will work out, I said, "No, I'm done." Only when you finally realize what you want to do, or what you don't want to do, will you truly find your passion. It's about being brave and speaking up. After ten years of gymnastics, I finally learned to speak up for myself; I wish I had done it sooner, which would have prevented a lot of pain.

In the fall of 2007, I fractured my spine in gymnastics, when I was only eleven years old. This event was traumatic because of the pain that surfaced, but most of my regret deals with what led up tothe injury. I spent twelve hours a week for four years in a beat up, old gym trying to master the sport of gymnastics. I didn't really spend much time being a kid, because I spent all of my time flipping through the air, walking on my hands, and training for competitions.

I broke my back in sixth grade because I didn't speak up and tell my coaches my back was hurting. I did the same skill over and over again, even though it strained my back, and I ended up snapping a part of my spine. Looking back, I realize that if you have something to say, just say it. It doesn't matter who you tell, as long as you don't keep everything bottled up inside. I still hadn't learned my lesson, though. It wasn't until three years, and four bone fractures later, that I finally spoke up and left gymnastics. I was done with the sport I had been trying to master since I was four years old. At the time it seemed like a tragic ending, but it was the beginning of a path that led me to become the person I am today. From this experience, I have one thing to say. Always have the courage to make a change, risk it all, and speak up for yourself. Though this may seem unnecessary or impossible at the time, to make a stagnant situation better, we must always move forward.

Before I fractured my spine, risking it all seemed irrational to me. So, I asked my dad why individuals would risk climbing the highest mountain in the world: Mount Everest. The idea seemed ridiculous to me because in every movie and documentary I'd seen, a bunch of people had died and suffered on the way to the summit of the mountain. His answer was, "Because they can" and it wasn't until I fractured my spine that I realized exactly what he meant.

To achieve great heights, we must risk it all sometimes, start over, and give it everything we've got, though we may not succeed. Ken Kesey once described in his book *One Flew Over the Cuckoo's Nest* the struggle McMurphy takes in betting he can lift a panel that is thousands of pounds. "His whole body shakes with the strain as he tries to lift something he knows he can't lift, something everybody knows he can't lift." Life is about trying, though you may not succeed. It's about giving it your all every second of every day and hoping that one day that work pays off in finding your gift and your passion. I like to think it will.

I'll leave you with a quote of my own, now that I have found my voice. "As one road ends, another one will always begin. So embrace the chaos, and enjoy the ride."

Seny lives in Castro Valley, CA

Making a Difference

Anyone who thinks they are too small to make a difference has never tried to fall asleep with a mosquito in the room.

~ Dalai Lama

Every year near the end of October, my daughter Jenny's piano teacher Mary turns 89. I had always assumed she simply forgot how old she was, or just didn't want to admit she was turning 90, and I questioned her sanity each passing year. How could someone forget their birthday? Mary doesn't even bother to remember the day of her birth. It's simply another passing day – with new opportunities and new chances to become a different person, just like any other day.

On this birthday, the student in the lesson before my daughter was a young boy who had just finished his tutoring, and he packed up his books and was ready to leave. He then whispered something in the air, "Oh Mary, I wanted to say Happy Birthday". The wise woman looked up from her chair, cleared her throat and whispered gently, "Oh, is it my birthday? I completely forgot." My daughter marched over to the piano bench, and Mary whispered in her ear "Guess what, Jenny, I turn 89 today."

This piano lesson was different, though. In fact, there was hardly any piano playing at all. Mary and Jenny were talking about which colleges she was going to apply to, then Mary took us on a journey of her life. From her rough childhood with strict parents, to earning a PhD in music at UC Berkeley; through this discussion I realized she isn't lacking in her cognitive abilities at all. She had lived a full and industrious life and was quietly proud of all that she had accomplished.

Mary told Jenny that she will conquer the world someday because she spends her time carefully and meaningfully, and has used her days to make herself a well-rounded individual. "Other people don't do this nowadays", says Mary.

Mary's stories taught me that it doesn't matter how long you've lived, but rather how you have spent your time here and how it has affected others. I am like Mary in a lot of ways; living with a positive attitude each day and looking forward to the future, and I still strive to emulate the effect she has had on others. My positivity shines at work when I collaborate with others, share ideas, share a smile, and I know many people appreciate my style. It also gleams at other times in everyday life, as I try to spread cheerfulness and positivity each day because to me that is the best way to live. I smile at strangers to make their day a better one, and I am often rewarded because many of them smile back at me.

Now that I am on the verge of retiring, I am taking stock of what I have learned and how I have impacted others. It's important to me to not stop here, as life is just beginning rather than coming to some sort of conclusion. Finances required me to keep a good job that paid well so that I could contribute to buying a house, supporting our family and sending our daughters to college; and for those opportunities I am grateful. At this time, however, the point has come for me to broaden my perspective and see how I can influence people in a different way, and in a way that is more important to me as an individual.

Kindness, empathy, connectivity and gratitude are the things that I work toward being better at each day, and hope that others will do the same thing. One day I was standing in line at the grocery store and the woman behind me was very stressed and looked like she could use someone to talk to. She told me that she was caring for her sister who was going through chemo, and her days were very busy with caregiving tasks. The line was long so we talked for a while; after we checked out I walked her to my car and gave her a copy of the book entitled Think Positive/Live Happy. This is the first book in which one of my stories was published, and she was so thankful for the positive gesture that she nearly cried. This was a good thing I could do in a given day - share my sense of optimism with someone who needed it.

When I was a child, I was fearless, confident and felt that with enough personality, anything is possible. I found exotic lands and exotic peoples from books; my imagination about what this world could offer to someone who grabbed a hold of opportunities to develop them into something useful was my main goal even as a youngster. This carefree spirit of possibilities is what I'm trying to recover and encourage.

Now that I think about it, I realize why birthdays aren't important. I try to make each day count and stand up for what I believe in. My husband and I have created a family that will forever be our most valued possession. I'm happy with my life, content each day I live, look forward to the future, and that's all that really matters. Age doesn't represent intelligence or knowledge, but rather just a period of time that someone has lived. Every day I think about things I can do to make the world a better place.

I plan on continually growing my gratitude just like Mary. Observing Mary's enthusiasm and graceful, ageless life fills me with abundance and life-affirming actions. I know that I will have a positive impact on people, perhaps in imperceptible ways or with some kind words or my big smile. I am happy to make a difference.

Carol Lake lives in the Bay Area

Meteor Showers

The Optimist sees the donut, the pessimist sees the hole.

~ Oscar Wilde

There's something so spectacular about watching streaks of light fly across the night sky. This phenomenon seems simple from such a great distance, and it's hard to fathom that the little flashes in the sky are actually meteors millions of miles away. Things aren't always what they seem. They can be distorted by distance, by time, and even by past experiences.

My best friend and I try to see the meteor showers whenever we can. My fondest memory of watching a meteor shower was only a few years ago. We packed up some snacks, brought a blanket, loaded up on warm clothes, and hiked up to the top of the hill that's on the top of my street. I remember the frigid air against my face, and the fear I felt as we ascended the staircase and path to the top of the hill at around midnight. I couldn't imagine what was hiding in the brush – Snakes? Raccoons? Murderers? We ventured on, though, and witnessed something beautiful that I hadn't truly understood until now.

Flashes of light were soon flying across the sky. Some

were short, some were longer, and some streaks of light were so bright you could watch them light up the night sky for just a moment. I recall feeling at peace for a moment, because life was so much more than the little things I was worried about at the time. In that moment, it was all about what was beyond Earth – everyday struggles seemed meaningless as I watched the rare phenomenon before me.

When I look at it now, I see the meteor shower differently. It's not so much about gaining perspective, but about how things aren't always as they seem. That tiny light across the sky was actually a massive meteor burning up in the atmosphere, but at the moment it seemed harmless. I guess it's human nature to see things differently – we all come from different backgrounds, have different stories to tell, and have different thought patterns. The meteor shower reminded me that a situation can be seen from many different viewpoints, and that maybe one is more realistic than another.

I've always had a problem with overthinking. Ever since I was a little kid I've taken situations I've been in, and overanalyzed them to the point of exhaustion. Don't get me wrong, thinking about what you've been through and future obstacles is a good thing, but when it gets to the point of unhealthy repetition, it needs to stop. I guess what I'm trying to say is that I've always escalated things in my mind, and I keep forgetting that from an outside perspective, my new views can seem unrealistic and unhealthy. That's why I like the meteor showers – I'm constantly reminded that something that seems so small right in front of me is actually a much more complex phenomenon. But is it better to see the flash of light as a streak across the sky, or as a massive meteor burning up in the atmosphere?

I believe there is a positive side to seeing things as both simple and complex, to an extent. It's great to take difficult situations, and simply let them pass, forget about them, and move on to the future. There's something to be said though, about trying to truly understand a situation, to the point that you learn something from it. Maybe it's about finding a middle ground – not simply letting situations pass you by, but also not dwelling and overanalyzing them to the point where you can't stop thinking about it.

A meteor flashes through the sky, but my best friend doesn't see it.

I went to class and tripped over my own shoe only to make an embarrassment of myself. I thought about it for the next two weeks, when in reality, nobody even remembered it.

A meteor flashes through the sky, but I don't see it.

I got a B on a calculus exam that I studied extremely hard for, but I'm upset because I thought I could get a better grade. The class average was a C minus.

A faint meteor flashes through the sky, and my friend and I stare in awe at what actually turned out to be an airplane.

My gymnastics coach told me I did a good job, but she also told that to all of the other gymnasts too. I must not be a good gymnast if everyone else is good too.

A meteor lights up the whole sky, but I say it wasn't as bright as the one two minutes ago.

I got into a great college but all I could think about was how I didn't do as well on the entrance exams as I should have. Maybe I would've gone to a better school.

We all see different situations in a different light, whether it be as a meteor or as a positive or negative situation. What I've learned is to open my mind to other viewpoints. Open my mind to the idea that I could be completely wrong about something. That something may not be what it seems. If you open your world to this possibility, you begin to question the negativity in your head, and really think about what is realistic and what is not. So, is it better to see the tiny streak across the sky, or the meteor crashing and burning into the atmosphere? Maybe it's to see both, and understand that both are a possibility. Whichever one makes you learn something, though, is the one you should follow.

Seny lives in Castro Valley, CA

The Fragility of Life

Life is fragile. We are not guaranteed a tomorrow so give it everything you've got.

~ Tim Cook

We all remember the day Ally went missing. Her 15-year-old face showed up on every news channel, every street corner, and blue ribbons were put up around the neighborhood signifying the hope that she would come home. She never did.

Ally was a star student, athlete, pianist, and a good friend to many. She seemed like the happiest sophomore in high school – she even skipped a grade due to her intelligence and was always seen smiling. A few weeks before her disappearance my best friend recalled seeing Ally in a classroom and could remember nothing but her "bright face and lighthearted wave". I had watched Ally grow from a small kindergartener to a sophomore, losing track of her along the way. What nobody knew, though, was that Ally was hiding a big secret.

When the news came out that she was last seen in the morning at our high school, removing her books from her locker, everyone began to think the worst. Records were found on her computer that indicated she may have been traveling to San Francisco alone, and when her bike was found in a field nearby the bridge, a frantic search began. I remember searching the creek near my house with my friend, and we were dead silent. All we could think of was the fact that our classmate would never come home, and that maybe she had planned this all out. She was incredibly smart, of course.

Everyone would watch the news every day. I remember pictures of a happy, young girl with freckles and white teeth and how they searched every lake, every cranny of our town, every part of San Francisco where she could possibly be staying, but nothing was found. Eventually, the video from the Golden Gate Bridge was released. A video of her walking across the bridge, alone, the day she was last seen, was released on television. We then knew that Ally probably wasn't going to be coming home. She had jumped from the bridge, ending her life.

I remember the accusations on the parents, the teary-eyed faces of the children in my classes who were just a little too young to understand the horror of the situation, and the great grief that spread across our little town. A vigil was held for Ally, but I didn't go. I guess I was just too shocked, and didn't want to believe that she was gone. I wanted to change something – maybe if I had gotten closer to her, I could have prevented her death. Nobody saw the depressed, lonely girl through those eyes and a great smile. The most horrifying part of the whole story was that nobody saw it coming. She had such a bright future, but she was suffering so much.

I go to Ally's bench a lot nowadays. They built it for her a few months after she went missing. When it was put in place, a group of 100 people gathered around the beautiful new bench, and flowers were placed on it for her. We all could only hope that she could see how much she was being missed. I like to think of Ally because she gives me perspective in my own life. Upon her disappearance, hundreds of people, some she knew, and some she didn't, worked endlessly together to bring her home. I saw unity within a group of people which I had not seen before. She affected so many people, and upon her passing, each and every person she had blessed her smile with had great grief. Whether it was a classmate, teacher, friend, friend of a friend, parent of a classmate, or even a random stranger – they showed up for her.

You never really think about how much you affect others until you see a community form to mourn the loss of a loved one. When I observed this, I began to think about all the people who would care if I was gone, and who would be hurting if they could never speak to me again. It was horrifying, really, how much of an effect one individual can have on those around them. I began to imagine how my family, my best friends, and my teachers would react if it was my face that had shown up on the television that day. They probably would've all come together to bring me home as well.

Ally and I had a lot in common. I didn't know her that well, but we were both studious and tended to get overwhelmed with the world. I think of her often when I have thoughts of running away, or worse. Sometimes I like to think I stay alive for those I love. Not only would it hurt for me to never see them again, but I am sure they would be devastated if they never got to see me again, either.

Ally is a fleeting memory to many, but she will always be with me. At the young age of 15, I was forced to understand the idea of death, and the fragility of life. How simple it can be taken away, and how much we should appreciate every day we have on this earth. We should be thankful for the things she may no longer be able to see – like the beautiful sunrise and sunset in a small suburban town, or the refreshing chill of rain after a long drought. Maybe all of these things are Ally reaching out to us and reminding us to dance in the rain as well as the sunshine. Life may be hard, but it's about appreciating the little things that make life worth living.

Seny lives in Castro Valley, CA

Walking hand in hand

Alone we can do so little; together we can do so much.

~ Helen Keller

A number of years ago my parents, Vin and Dee, were taking a walk down by the Niagara River in Tonawanda, New York, with the summer breeze gently making sure that it was not too hot, with the birds chirping hello to all who passed. It is really nice in the summer there, and is also very cold and snowy in the winter. It's all about the balance between nature's contrasting elements, with each offering its own charm and significance.

Vin and Dee, ice cream cones in hand, had just come from Mississippi Mudds across the street, which was a popular burger and ice cream restaurant in town. When they walked anywhere, they always held hands. My parents were both on the small side and were of Italian descent. They had been married for 69 years, and looked like the cutest couple.

The young people working at the restaurant were amazed that they still held hands and seemed so in love. "How can I find that kind of partnership?", they wondered. This was not the first time a stranger asked them that question; it had happened many times previously.

Walking hand in hand was a symbol of their affection and a willingness to navigate life's journey together, and the young adults wanted a guidebook on how to make that special spark happen for themselves. How to create the magic that glues a couple together and bonds them for life. Good communication and listening is often the glue that holds people together; when a person is listened to, it makes them feel valued.

Vin and Dee had known each other since they were freshmen in high school. They had been friends and dated a little for quite some time, and one day Mom was walking down the school hallway in front of my Dad and she turned off into her next classroom; my dad's classroom was further down the hall. At that time, my Dad had a premonition: he thought to himself – "Someday, I'm going to marry that girl."

Vin and Dee graduated from high school in 1947, and they were still dating in 1950. One day Vin said to Dee, "Should I buy a new car, or should we get married?" Dee was startled, so at the time she answered, "You should buy a new car." So Vin bought a new 1950 Studebaker.

After he bought the Studebaker, Vin went to a small jewelry store on Niagara Street, and he bought a modest, sparkling engagement ring for $200. The next time Vin and Dee went on a date, they were in an Italian restaurant/bar that served burgers and pasta and other simple food, and was a local place where people could meet.

Vin put the box with the ring in front of Dee. "What do you say?", Vin asked assertively. Dee gave a simple answer - "OK."

They had known each other for a long time and were ready for the next step. Then Vin said "I think I should ask your father if I can marry you." So he asked Grandpa, and Grandpa said OK. This is how their 69-year marriage began.

Vin grew up as an only child, and he liked the way he grew up because it was in a very calm and supportive household. They were pretty poor but always had enough money to put food on the table. Learning to read when he was 4 was one of the best things he ever did, and reading has always been an important part of his life.

Vin is very inquisitive, and over time he became an observer. This perspective invites individuals to engage in the world in a contemplative and reflective manner. He always felt that it was important to be nice to people and to consider the feelings of other people, which is a fundamental aspect of building meaningful connections with others.

Dee grew up in a large, Italian family and had 4 siblings. Her father had immigrated from Sicily with his parents when he was 12, and Dee's family did a little better financially than my dad's had. She was pretty and quite reserved; some classmates thought she was stuck up, but she was just quiet. Dee was a good mother, managed the household, and was creative and artistic. She was stubborn and never gave up until things were the way she wanted them to be.

Vin and Dee had a successful marriage for 69 years, thought that the success of a marriage is focused on compromise, and compromise was a part of their life philosophy. Whether it be agreeing on which movie to see or which parenting skill to use, they always worked in unity. Both parties have to share in giving in so that an agreement can be made (no running tally was kept of who gave in more often). The important part was being open to alternatives.

They felt that you can believe in what you are saying, but as right as you think you are, you could be wrong. You can't always be right, and you don't have to be right all the time. It's important to put yourself in the other person's shoes and look at it from their perspective.

Our family always operated as a team, with Dad working long hours and Mom often taking the brunt of handling my two brothers and myself. Every time Dad would come home from work, though, we three kids would wait for his arrival, and whether we were in the house or playing outside down the street, we would always run out, jump on Dad and welcome him home. That's the type of family we were and are: always supporting each other, working together, and making sure we are all doing well.

My mom passed away several years ago, but my dad is still mentally active and reads all the time. A good answer to the young people who question my parents about how they made it work so well for 69 years and why they still held hands - holding hands is a good show of compromise, where both parties are thinking "I'm willing to listen." Walking hand in hand symbolizes their love, unity, and shared experiences, and creates a comforting and secure connection.

Carol Lake lives in the Bay Area

The Essence of Life

The energy of the mind is the essence of life.

~ Aristotle

"Mommy, mommy, can you help me with this?" our 5-year-old daughter asks me as she tugs on my pants with one hand and holds her coloring book in her other hand.

"Sure Honey, let me finish rinsing this glass."

Just then our other two daughters walk in the kitchen and ask for their magic markers. I put the glass in the dish rack and remove the magic markers from the cabinet where they're stored. Their eager small hands grab for the markers as soon as I place them on the kitchen table. They've already staked their position at the table and are anxious to create their own world of polka dot houses, purple dogs and brick red leaves.

Before returning to the sink to finish the dishes, I take a few moments to watch our girls playfully color their pictures. I think about how they're creating their own piece of artwork in life. They're so young, so innocent. They have their whole lives ahead of them and a lot of potential to be whomever they choose to be.

Jenny, age 6, could be a teacher or a psychologist when she becomes older. Our second daughter, Julie, is in kindergarten now. She's showing great potential in being a debater or maybe she'll surprise us and become involved in medicine. Maddy is just 3 years old. She may simply prefer to be a stay-at-home mom, and who knows what skills will develop out of her bright, young mind. Whatever our girls decide, the possibilities are limitless. It's magical, almost, this gift that's given to each and every one of us to develop ourselves into whatever type of person we want to be and contribute whatever we are able to society.

My life has been full of challenging obstacles, and I have spent much time overcoming them. When I was 18, I was walking across the street, was hit by a car, and thrown into a severe coma. Recovering from my coma taught me to fight for what I want despite the difficulties and the challenges of doing so and despite the risk of failure, for no dream will come true on its own. Dreams worth having will not give themselves to us without a fight. This is the lesson I wanted to pass on to our children.

Sometimes it's necessary to alter one's dreams just a little bit to fit reality. For example, my physical limitation of processing abstract qualitative information was real, as made known to me in various positions throughout my academic and professional careers. So I adjusted myself and found another means to success in a more quantitative role, namely, one in financial management. My goals remained the same and I continued to pursue them. And though the road to them may have been longer and a little more difficult to travel, I never took my eyes off them.

Life is a gift, a very precious one, to be lived to its fullest. Such is how I have chosen to live my life; with this in mind, with living well as my mission. I have spent my years developing myself into someone I can be proud of, taking advantage of this gift to live it to its fullest extent. I wish that for each of our girls.

Now it makes sense—we are all born into a network, a family environment, and not as single individuals. We are interconnected and what affects one family member affects all. A family unit is not limited to a biological family. For some a family network may be a church or a synagogue family, a social club, or even a recovery support group. In some cases, a work group.

Working with others—whether it be with family members, co-workers, friends—it's important to keep up the link we have with others, and the link we have with society. Sadly, many people have withdrawn from their relationships with others because of hurts and disappointments. Others have become engrossed in their own troubles to the point that they've isolated themselves. But it's those relationships that keep us going, make us thrive in the face of adversity, and give us a reason for living.

Some people can face a personal loss and never recover. The loss of one's legs, eyesight, or a hand can devastate some people beyond being able to come back and be productive again. But to some people, being "disabled" does not mean they still can't lead a productive life. Everyone who is "disabled" is not if they are still connected to society and to each other.

I have found that what I've been through sets me apart in this way. I've experienced an awakening by way of a deep sleep. I don't take things for granted and I have learned that I can do just
about anything I choose to do. My goals are realistic, yet high enough to motivate me to work to reach them. My goals are truly an essential part of me, of my life, for they are the means to furthering myself, to growing and learning and strengthening myself.

But in addition to seizing every opportunity I can to learn and to grow myself, a goal of mine is to help others further themselves too. This has become just as important a goal to me as helping myself, and is partly rooted in my awareness of and appreciation for all the help and support I received from doctors, nurses, friends, and family at a time when my life and my future depended upon it.

I have come to realize that the true essence, the true value of life is in the journey. The successes and defeats of winning one battle and losing the next provide the incentive to keep moving and to keep pushing. It is the journey towards them that makes life a challenge and what makes it great. It takes a lot of work, but the best things in life are often those that are earned.

The dishes are complete, and the girls are wrapping up their art projects. I look at my family one last time. I'm so lucky to have been able to come this far, to build such a wonderful family unit. I smile. I hope that my husband and I can instill in our children the knowledge that the real essence of life is in the journey— the work we do to make something happen.

Carol Lake lives in the Bay Area

Acknowledgments

The world is a better place thanks to people who empower others to grow and become the best version of themselves.

To my loving husband and three wonderful daughters – I am so thankful to each of you for the family we have built and the support we provide to each other.

To my mom and dad who were by my side as I fought to regain my abilities; to my brother Paul who visited each day at the hospital with his positive energy and kept me company; to my brother Rob, who among other things, played a pivotal role by engaging in spirited pinochle games with me every day to help get my mind back in order.

To my good friend Angela Hom who was my continuous inspiration when I started this writing quest; to my friend Jeane Oribello who consulted and partnered with me to format my vision and create the initial stories.

To Suzanne James-Peters and Celeste Palmer, loyal friends who are my partners in the pursuit to help TBI survivors reclaim their joy; to my new friend Breanne Boyle, who wrote such a lovely story; to the entire Bridging the Gap TBI support group, who gave me the motivation to share these uplifting stories.

To Danette Mitchell, who helped me with my original manuscript to tell my initial story.

I want to say thank you to everyone who ever said anything positive to me. I heard it all, and it meant something.